Prayers for Our Day

E. LEE PHILLIPS

Prayers for Our Day

Morning * Midday * Evening

John Knox Press
ATLANTA

Library of Congress Cataloging in Publication Data

Phillips, E. Lee.
  Prayers for our day.

  1. Prayers. I. Title.
BV245.P46 1982   242'.2   81–82349
ISBN 0–8042–2583–4 (pbk.)   AACR2

He went to his house where he had windows
in his upper chamber open toward Jerusalem;
and he got down upon his knees
three times a day and prayed and gave
thanks before his God.

Daniel 6:10 (RSV, italics added)

In loving memory of
MARILYN JOYCE BROWN
The inspiration of a lifetime

Contents

Spring

In Spring every creature that was asleep, wakens; everything shut, opens; every seed hiding in the ground emerges. Sunshine works this magic, wakening animals to scamper in the woods, opening flowers to bloom, bringing trees to bud, causing brooks to dance again, opening human beings to the expansive outdoors. Birds chatter, and it is not about the past but the future— a message of hope and faith about how much warmer it is getting, how much there is to do. We get the message too, you and I, and want to stay outside a little longer to see if in favorite forest haunts the mayapples have returned. Are the daffodils blinking sunlight and winking at rain-drops, are the dainty wild columbines holding court among the high rocks on yonder ridge? Spring is never better than in the green glades of variegated light where the sounds of the happy populace are heard, where every evening ballet takes place at the hidden freshwater spring.

Spring enters in hide-and-go-seek fashion; warmth is here and then it is gone. It is a fickle season. Days can move from loveliness to terror in hours. Flood and wind and raging storm can devastate.

Spring calls the Christian heart to the season of Lent. The Life of Christ is studied. Eventually the journey from the town of Bethany, the rejoicing of a triumphal entry into Jerusalem to moments of sad drama is made. Jesus is seen, sold out, forsaken, falsely accused, unjustly tried, savagely beaten, mercilessly crucified. It was the unexpected, Jerusalem's noon sun wreathed in shadows, with thick black clouds, rolling thunder and terrible light-ning pounding the earth, splitting tremors in the land when The King of the Jews breathed His last breath. More was rent than the veil of the temple, but the veil was enough! What began in the heart of God and was sealed in obedience on Calvary's Cross was victoriously vali-dated in the Resurrection. It was the most important progression in the history of the planet and it is still going on, this sharing of an Easter Message where the cataclys-mic upheavel of a springtime day, ultimately conquered sin and wrought salvation to all who will believe. Resur-rection, Life, Hope: Spring echoes the grace of God and mirrors the profoundest images of heaven we have.

Morning

Holy God, who comes in such an hour as I think not, in such a way as I least expect, in such a manner as I cannot predict; deliver me from all falseness and deception, all self-seeking and vain display, from all callousness and closedness, from all vanity and intemperance, from all insensitivity and hard-heartedness.

Deliver me from:
the pride that demands exception,
the worry that negates faith,
the depression that clouds options,
the jealousy that destroys character,
the envy that ruins life,
the deception that distorts truth,
the falseness that mocks concern,
the affluence that forgets poverty,
the criticism that assumes judgment,
the hatred that destroys relationships,
the apathy that weakens faith.

There is in me selfishness that would usurp the rights of others and distort Thy will. Forgive my lack of concern and lead me to the insight that merges reality and behavior into a God-honoring faith. Rectify me in Thy counsel. Pardon my sin. Restore my soul. Realign me in Thy will through faith in Christ Jesus, my Lord. Amen.

Midday

Creator of the morning and the night,
Of noon and afternoon and gentle evening;
As Thou hast led me in the morning,
Guide me through the afternoon.
Give me the grace to love Thee with a whole heart;
That in pursuing Thee I may find Thee,
In finding Thee I may serve Thee,
In serving Thee in the difficult places,
I may find myself and point others
To the Christ who finds us all in love.
Amen.

Evening

Creating God, Serene, Mystical, Righteous;
hold me longer in the glory of Thy Presence:
Unerring in judgment,
Unfaltering in mercy,
Purposeful in Creation,
Compassionate in grace.

For my earthly vision is dimmed by the things of
this world and I desire Thy holiness. My heart clamors
after Thy courts: in Thy dwelling place is my peace. My
soul longs for Thy counsel. My joy is the keeping of Thy
law. Day and night I praise Thee and my voice rises to
magnify Thee.

Bestow vision to my weary eyes.
Give purpose to my seeking heart.
Set my feet in paths of righteousness.
Let my hands do good work.
Let my mind feed on thoughts of Thee.
Let my soul rejoice in Thee.
In strength may I not falter.
In faith may I not forsake.
In hope let me not despair.
In love keep and use me.

Through the long-awaited Messiah. Amen.

Morning

Almighty God, Savior and Guide, Open the eyes of my soul as I contemplate the passion of Christ. Reveal any stumbling sin, pierce any darkened motives, flood any covetous desires with shafts of holy light, consuming falseness, eradicating pride, transforming waning allegiance into dynamic faith.

I recall:
The memorial supper and prayer in the garden,
The kiss of betrayal and desertion of the disciples,
The false charges and flimsy trials,
The blood-thirsty mobs and unwarranted scourgings,
The crown of thorns and mocking soldiers,
The wooden Cross with three nails to hold Him,
The agony of dying and the last words,
The final breath and nature's cataclysmic upheaval.

Mature and deepen me by the willing sacrifice of The Faithful Son.
   By conviction draw me,
      By example challenge me,
         By redemption strengthen me,
            To share more perfectly The Name
               I have never felt worthy to name
                  But by Thy grace I have the privilege
                     To name and proclaim
                        Jesus Christ, Lord of all. Amen.

Midday

Bread enough for every day,
Hope sustaining in all sorrow.
Strength enough to live today,
Grace sufficient for tomorrow.
Light enough to see the way,
Peace no doubt can steal or borrow.
Joy enough to give away,
Love has met me: Lord I follow!
Amen.

Evening

Eternal God, most Holy. I remember this day all persons who search for peace amid struggle and have not found it:

Those who are haunted by a former embarrassment, who cannot forget the past or live peaceably in the present;

Those whose roads run counter to their parents, their friends, their conscience, their culture, their mates;

Those whose paths appear to wind in circles, eventuating in detours leading to alcoholic and marital dead ends;

Those who try to buy happiness and respectability;

Those who struggle for identity and those who with strong identity search for acceptance;

Those who found what they sought and do not want it, cannot live with it, and want more;

Those who would rather suffer;
Those who fear death;
Those who can't find home.

We are all lost and frightened creatures without Thee, O Lord. Where would I be were it not for Thy promises and Presence? In Thy grace is my sustenance, in Thy will my direction, in Thy love my hope, through Jesus, my Savior. Amen.

Morning

Lord God, Omnipotent, I pray for those who see the day lying before them and are discouraged. Events have merged to bring difficulty into their lives and instead of accepting these problems as a challenge they seem more imbalanced now than ever. Nothing in past experience quite matches the challenges that confront them. Waking means making painful decisions and they would rather not face the day on those terms. No alternative seems to exist which they prefer, yet reality presses in with its demands. Their faith is sorely tested. Their spirits are low; patience is at a premium. They feel unequal to the task and dread living with the consequences. They feel in a bind if they do and in a bind if they don't, and this is the part of life they find most difficult to accept.

It is not to others they feel they can turn now; that phase seems to be over. It is up to them. It is a personal matter, or it is a result of actions they gave full assent to that now have returned to haunt them, or it is a catastrophic event over which they had no control. In innocence they must suffer what someone else has caused to happen.

Lord, Mighty and Strong, lead them to the strength that never fails. Give them to realize:

When Thou seemest most remote, Thou wast never closer;

When circumstances confuse, Thou art not unmindful of their purpose;

When tragedy seems unbearable, Thou art ever present to strengthen;

When injustice runs unchecked, Thy judgment cannot be overwhelmed;

When punishment comes swiftly, Thou chastenest out of love;

When grief stings, comfort was never less available;

When temptation lures, help through prayer is possible;

When difficulty surrounds, Thy love is adequate to lead *through* the dark valley.

By The Spirit and The Son. Amen.

Midday

Lord, I am grateful for this day, the potential and privileges of it. May I make wise use of each hour. Let me not attribute to minor matters more importance than they deserve, nor exaggerate them or myself out of all proportion to reality. May I have the balance and perspective of The Master who discerned as no one else, the essential from the trivial and accomplished Thy perfect will. Amen.

Evening

Heavenly Father,
Thy greatness is to be proclaimed throughout the earth.
Thy mercy is greater than I can tell.
Thy judgments are just and right.
Thy mighty acts are beyond compare.
Thy Name is to be exalted and Thy power acknowledged.
Thy ordinances are true and Thy precepts to be obeyed.
In glory Thou dost reign and Thy righteousness is unto all peoples.
My soul delights in Thee, my heart longs for Thy counsel.
Encompass me with Thy compassion and guide me by Thy statutes.
Hide Thy Word in my heart and let me be jealous of Thy law.
Withdraw not Thy watchcare from me nor leave me to my own counsel.
Stir my heart to obedience, let my soul sing Thy praise.
Thou art all Holiness and in Majesty doest Thou reign.
Hear my prayer and save me by Thy Strong Right Arm.
Amen.

Morning

Almighty God, in whose will my life finds purpose, in whose love I take direction, in whose grace I am brought to saving faith, may my first thought on waking be in praise of Thee and my last thought before sleeping be gratitude to Thee for Thy blessings to me. I am grateful for those realities of faith that have kept me from:

parking by my failures,
nursing my ills,
flaunting my achievements,
giving in to despair,
coveting what is another's,
ignoring suffering,
missing simplicity,
bartering my soul for trinkets.

Match my dedication with my deeds. Wrap my desires around Thy will and lead me to a deep understanding of Holy trust.

Spirit prepare me,
Prayer shape me,
Love surround me,
Faith prod me,
Hope take me,
Christ meet me
In service today.
Amen.

Midday

Wise Father, grace me with wisdom in speech today.
May I weigh my words carefully.
Let me mean what I say and say what I mean and listen attentively.
Allow me silence until the opportune moment comes.
May I be quick to hear, thoughtful in reply and slow to anger.
Let me recall again the Master's example who encouraged faith, praised compassion, rebuked when rebuke was needed, pinpointed sin, and spoke The Words of Life.
What may I speak for Thee today, Holy God? Amen.

Evening

Merciful God, who sees the heart and understands the fluctuations of the soul, who rejoices in praise and worship, empathizing beyond human awareness with every distress; I pray for those who suffer from loneliness tonight:

> Who travel in far-away territory and feel the walls closing in on them;
>
> who wrestle with vexing temptation when they are alone in distant places;
>
> who have reached an agonizing decision and left on a one-way ticket;
>
> who feel their marriage crumbling;
>
> who have watched their friends die and fear they may be alone in the end;
>
> who never felt wanted;
>
> who have been abused and cannot trust;
>
> who blame everyone else;
>
> who cannot sustain relationships;
>
> who are surrounded by friends and cannot feel their love.

In recalling the separateness that comes from being in the minority yet knowing you are right, I visualize Jesus standing firm while others falsely accused or defected. Bring me to understand that the ultimate victory over sin came from the loneliest encounter in history: Christ on a Cross.

Lord Jesus, may I behold Thee this night on the throne of God, by the right side reigning in power, interceding in love, surrounded in majesty, filled with mercy, covered by glory. Rest me in Thy Lordship and bring me at last, into unhindered fellowship with Thee and the redeemed. For Thy name's sake. Amen.

Morning

This day begins and I begin with the thought of Thee, my God. Surround me, search me, immerse me in Thy will. Reflect to me the light of Christ.

So much can happen in a day:
Whom will I meet?
What news may affect me deeply?
What temptation may try me?
What problem may reoccur?
What burden will I be called to bear?
What challenge may inspire me?

God of all things large and small, who numbers the hairs of my head and knows my coming in and going out; lead me to a resilient faith.

I pause to remember in prayer many persons whose work touches the lives of others:
teachers, who open minds to truth;
writers, who depict life as it is;
artists, who show us as we are;
doctors, who aid the healing process;
ministers, who break the Bread of Life;
therapists, who help cohese our separate selves;
comedians, who help us laugh at ourselves.

Through the influence of such persons as these, my life has been enriched. May I, in work and leisure, share both gifts of myself and gifts of faith, thus authenticating the grace that binds me to Thy Everlasting Love. Amen.

Midday

God of Salvation, I pause in this Lenten noon hour, recalling that at this hour centuries ago, a crude cross held the living body of Jesus Christ until He died. My tendency is to make that moment prettier than it was, to believe my sin was not that costly. Let me not run from the reality of that day nor forsake its implications in my conduct. Hold me longer at the foot of the cross while the clouds gather and the rains come and breath leaves my Savior. Then fill me with the Love that will not ignore a Son forever. Amen.

Evening

O God, my Father, as I pause to praise Thee in this evening hour, give me to realize The Risen Christ here with me in this room. Allow that I may speak to Thee in the consciousness of Thy Presence. Let the material and temporal give way to the spiritual and eternal. How often I have done everything else but bring this picture of Thy Son into focus. During this time of prayer, let me think on my Savior: the way He handled situations and came to the core of the matter; the way He noticed others and helped them delineate truth from fiction, faith from self-indulgence. May I see anew what Jesus meant in laying down one's life for others, in going the second mile, in seeking The Kingdom of God and His righteousness first. Fill me with the tough mettle of His meekness. Shape me in the strength of His courage; embolden me with the audacity of His faith. Let me not hide my talents in the ground but share them, remembering His words. "Greater works than I do, will you do."

Is there something I ought to give up,
someone I need to seek out,
some sin I need to relinquish,
some Scripture I need to internalize,
some flaw in character that needs Thy grace?

May I see myself through the Savior's eyes? May I know Jesus Christ as I have not yet known Him in the power of His Resurrection and the fellowship of His suffering? Thy will be done. Amen.

Morning

Generous God, I bless Thee for that within me which cries out to Thee, which desires Thy counsel, which seeks Thy will and lingers in the quiet of Thy Presence. Thou didst plant within me the need to pray and I pray for the Life of Christ Jesus within me, that it might be strengthened and brought to fruition.

These quiet moments in prayer have brought me to consider the larger world about me and how I may relate to that world in Christocentric faith. Because I have been called to act as salt effecting society with Thy redemptive power, these are areas where my discipleship calls me to intelligent concern.

How can the principles of Christ affect a technological society where the blessings of science are emphasized over the blessings of The Spirit?

How can Christian ethics effect bureaucracies and multinational corporations that often tend to overlook the individual while serving the masses?

How can the gospel message be presented by the media so as to lead to depth commitment, contemplative personal theology, church involvement, and spiritual maturity?

How may I exercise my stewardship of the earth in maintaining ecological balance in preserving wildlife and natural resources?

How may I apply the eternal truths of Jesus Christ wherever in the universe the human heart beats?

How may I act in courageous faith to rid the earth of hunger, prejudice, and war?

I am mindful today of the precarious state of my world that can so easily be harmed by polluted water, toxic chemicals, nuclear power misused, poisioned air, denial of human freedoms, and none of these problems so characteristic of the tension of our time has a simple solution. Do not let that keep me from struggling with them and seeking to be a peacemaker who is part of the solution and not part of the problem. Through The Christ of The Ages, I pray. Amen.

Midday

Prayer comes on silent feet
The waiting heart to dress.
Prayer brings the truth of God
All weary lives to bless.
Prayer leads the burdened heart
Sin's failures to confess.
Prayer, the soul's sincere communion
Joins with God in deepest union.

Loving Lord, join me in unison with Thy perfect will through Jesus, my Savior. Amen.

Evening

Gracious Lord, Source of my life; in gratitude I praise Thy watchcare over me and the abundant life that is mine in faith. Often I stumble and fall. Undergird me:

lest I steal the birthrights of my sisters and brothers to obtain power that is not mine;

lest I wander in the wilderness of disobedience and see not Thy light by day and fire by night;

lest I watch the walls of faith crumble and find my heart overrun by sin;

lest I sell myself to the slavery of the flesh and awaken imprisoned to my alleged liberties;

lest I wrestle with an angel of mercy and come away unblessed.

Teach me to be more observant.

Teach me to be more sensitive to the Providence of God.

Teach me obedience.

Let me be meek and humble.

Let me be courageous and trusting.

Let me be ennobled and edified in spiritual maturity.

This day has been filled with opportunities; Thy grace aided me in understanding them. Did I miss that warm affirmation that meant so much? Has duty brought out new strengths in me? Have moments of weakness taught me to trust? Has the sacrifice of Christ Jesus fired me to new dedication and commitment? Almighty God, Thou hast met me and my soul rejoices. Praise to Thee Father, Who with The Holy Spirit and Christ Jesus, hath led me to life abundant and hope eternal. Amen.

Morning

Lord of Creation, who gives life and provides the strength to live it in simple trust, I rely on Thee; I recall the "in between times" in my life and take these moments at the start of this day to pray for all who face transitions between:

dreaming and doing,
continuing and finishing,
short sightedness and wisdom,
wanting and needing,
participation and abstinence,
immaturity and commitment,
doubt and belief,
weakness and strength,
curiosity and salvation.

I recall the courage of Jesus Christ who came to the realization of His purpose in this life and did not turn from the cruelty of the Cross. He was dishonored by those who should have honored Him. He was rejected by the very ones who should have accepted Him. In His hour of greatest need, His disciples fell asleep. On the Cross, He had the presence of mind to speak with a criminal about Paradise; then, with His compassionate heart perfectly in tune with Thy will, He bridged the transition between sin and death, and opened the way to glory for all who will believe.

I praise Thee, Lord, for that Cross, arched between heaven and earth. Cleanse me in the blood of the Lamb and, Father, fill me with Thy love: the world needs it, help me to share it. For Jesus' sake. Amen.

Midday

Gracious Lord, save me from compromising convictions to obtain power only to find no joy in the exchange. Keep me from bargaining my soul for the fleeting pleasures of a world invaded by evil. Let me not approve of that which disapproves of Thee nor encourage that which denies Thy Lordship. May I choose to walk in the narrower paths of Love's devotion than the wide thoroughfares of sin's inducements. Give me the insight to discern these matters when opinion is divided and insight is required. In The Name of Christ who ate with sinners and sinned not. Amen.

Evening

Loving God, I cannot pray without recalling how I have strayed. I repent my failures in thought, word, and deed. Forgive and guide me.

Let me not stray so far that my influence does not reveal my faith, or that my belief fails to grapple with suffering.

Let me not fear to speak the propitious word that pinpoints the availability of salvation in Christ, for every person.

Let me not take lightly a regular time of prayer when I seek to consider the whole counsel of God revealed in Scripture and apply it to my heart.

Called to be a disciple, to witness and affirm in word and deed The Living Christ, I have too often gone other ways and ignored my Christian duty.

Forgive, Father, my awful lack, my hesitancy and petty rationalizations. Let me be involved in the evangelization of this world for the advancement of Thy Kingdom.

Merciful God,
Light of the faithful,
Strength to those who toil,
Sustenance to those who believe,
Deliverer of the tempted;

Speak to me in the quiet of the night.
Inform my mind, awake or asleep.
Be in my thoughts and in my dreams.
Let me rest in confidence and greet tomorrow renewed.
Through the wondrous power of The Lord Jesus Christ.
Amen.

Morning

O Divine Father, Source of my reflection,
Strength of my life, Origin of my hope; I pause to ponder
the words that surround my day, my use and misuse of
them, their power to lift or to destroy, to build or maim.
Forgive me, merciful Lord, the folly of things said which
would be better left unsaid:

heated words that accuse,
jealous words that hate,
unwarranted words that blame,
belittling words that taunt,
mean words that sour,
dishonest words that deny,
timid words that hide,
cheap words that disgrace,
thoughtless words that sear,
hasty words that harm.

Allow instead:

kind words that cheer,
uplifting words that inspire,
tender words that comfort,
wise words that guide,
affirming words that build,
forgiving words that heal,
encouraging words that challenge,
thoughtful words that redirect,
appropriate words that explain,
prayerful words that intercede.

May my words flow less from the heat of the
moment than from a heart disciplined by Thy will and
tempered by Thy Word. Through Him who is The Word
of Life. Amen.

Midday

Almighty God, hear my midday voice of gratitude for the knowledge of Thee that steadies me in crises,
undergirds me in storm and strengthens me in temptation. How often trying circumstances have pinpointed
grace that in less harried moments I had overlooked. Wed

my will more perfectly with Thy will and my ways with
the ways of righteousness through faith in The Perfect
Son. Amen.

Evening

    Righteous God,
I have wandered far from Thee.
In rebellion I have turned from the good Thou doest
   intend
And chosen the questionable Thou doest not intend for me.
Knowing the light, I chose darkness.
Walking the right road, I chose to detour.
Learning to trust, I succumbed to doubt.
Seeing Thy way, I chose my way.
Pursued by love, I kept my distance.
Having gone only part way and lapsed,
My commitment has become a pretense,
My example a mockery,
My faith a shambles.
Broken, defeated, and ashamed,
I come in contrition and utter my confession.
My sins have separated me from Thee,
Separate Thyself not from me.
Hear the depths of my penitence.
Stay the hand of Thy judgment against me.
Turn not Thy face from me.
Leave me not to my own devices.
Let me not remain in the conceit of my own choosings,
Nor in the mire of my own consequences.
Pluck me from the pit of my own misery.
Deliver me from the depths of my own folly.
Rescue me from the empty ways I have so vainly sought.
Cleanse, restore, and pardon me.
Then, may I rise renewed, proclaiming Thy mercy
And magnifying Thy great power,
O Lord of Hosts.
Amen.

Morning

Uncreated One, who art never confined except as Thou chooseth to be for Thy purposes, whose reach is beyond time and space, yet whose love reaches into every human heart; no day begins but what Thy watchcare goes before. No hour elapses without Thy knowledge. The birds of the air are known to Thee. The lilies of the field are sustained by Thee. The planets spin in their orbits because Thou hast so ordained them. Aware that no activity goes unnoticed:

I pray for those to whom outer space is familiar territory, who by training and preparation have chosen life above the earth to life on the earth, for whom confronting the mysteries of the universe is a realistic occupation. Their days are spent in close quarters, under precarious circumstances, often risking safety to do their work. Increase to those dependent on life-support systems the support through faith that never fails.

I pray for those to whom inner space, the world of the mind and psyche, is familiar territory, who by training and preparation have chosen to confront neurosis and psychosis as their occupation. May the listening, interpretation, analysis, and therapy of doctors of the mind lead to the wisdom of the soul. May illness find healing not only through insight but wholeness through faith in Jesus Christ.

I pray for those to whom limited space is familiar territory, who by age or circumstance are confined, for whom incarceration or hospitalization is a daily routine. Though restricted in movement, restrict not the power of the gospel to renew their minds in Thee and bring them peace.

Great God, Sovereign within, Ruler without, Creator and Lord of the universe; as the springtime dew rises in the heat of noonday, may my praise of Thee rise all through this day until at evening I may pause and praise Thee more. In Jesus' Holy Name. Amen.

Midday

I will sing praises unto The Lord, The God of my
salvation.
In the hour of trouble I would have hid had it not been for
Thy power.
Thy strength sustained me.
Thy light led me.
Thy word ordered my steps.
Thy counsel directed me.
Even now, Thy truth enables me to assume my
place in the world and by Thy lovingkindness to work
in joy and peace.
I will sing praises unto The Lord.
I will sing His praises forever. Amen.

Evening

This night I bring to Thy keeping, O Lord, the
welfare of my life, my soul, all I have done and thought
and hoped to do; my deeds, my dreams, my words, my
actions, my prayers before Thy throne. Hold also in Thy
tender care my family and friends and acquaintances,
those whom I have treated fairly and cared for sincerely,
those whom I treated unfairly and wronged. Forgive my
failings with others and restore my fellowship with them
and with Thee.

I intercede for those whose needs are almost too
painful for them to bear. Comfort those who go to bed
tonight with less faith than they have ever felt before
because circumstances have combined to unsteady them.
They look square into the face of disease that will not go
away, or injury that cannot be reversed, or relationships
permanently ruptured, or death inevitable, and find
themselves depressed and broken in heart.

Enter into their great hour of pain with Thy
Divine strength adequate for every need and allow the
accompanying silence in its own way to remind of The
Crucified Savior who understands.

Lend now Thy evening mercies to my rest. If
tomorrow I should rise from sleep to service here or in
glory, may it all be to Thy honor and The Savior's praise.
Amen.

Morning

Father, the day is not long upon me before faith is called to delineate between truth and falsehood. May the wisdom of the Scripture and sound reasoning combine to illumine all who have important choices to make between:

    ignorance and knowledge,
    moderation and abstinence,
    marriage and singleness,
    sanity and insanity,
    skepticism and commitment,
    violence and self-control,
    disobedience and cooperation,
    apathy and action.

Remind me of the faithfulness of Jesus, who faced paradox and ambiguity with unflinching courage, who in the choice between good and evil, routed sin and conquered death. Perplexities continue, life puzzles, yet Christ remains victorious. May I be edified and expanded today, by that which I hold and that which holds me fast in the faith of my Lord Jesus Christ. Amen.

Midday

Almighty God, at the midway point in my day, I recommit myself to Thee. In those duties where I have acted wisely in concert with others and Thy will, bring our combined efforts to fruition. And where, due to misunderstandings, our work has brought discord, forgive our erring ways. Let not the breach remain unbroken nor our smallness unforgiven. Bring us repentant to a better work, to build a better world for the sake of Christ and the Kingdom. Amen.

Evening

Almighty and Everlasting God,
How often I have prayed to Thee amiss,
Requesting what I did not need,
Expecting what I could not use,
Presuming what was not rightfully mine,
Failing to notice what was already mine,
Neglecting to prepare myself for what could be mine,
Allow that I might be content
Less with answers and more with communion,
Less with wants and more with needs,
Less with requests and more with obedience,
Desirous not of Thy blessings but only of Thee.

Give me to know when requests are not granted, I am
always heard and when in error prayers are worded
awry, the intent of the heart is always answered.

Where circumstances remain unchanged, Thou givest
strength to change attitudes toward circumstances.

When tragedy strikes, Thou canst work the limitation into
good for all who answer Thy call in Love.

Gracious Lord, who knowest better than I know
what is needful and what will bring me to embrace Thy
will more perfectly, hide me in the Mystery of Thyself and
shape me after Thy precepts that Thy Name may be
glorified, Christ Jesus honored, and others given to know
Thy unfettered Love. Amen.

Morning

Almighty God, whose mercy is still remembered, whose glory is still glimpsed, whose power is still felt, whose mighty acts are still known in the earth; my soul is alive with praise and exultant with adoration for Thy Guiding Hand. There are whispers of Thy Presence that cannot be denied; there are stirrings of Thy purposes that cannot be ignored, there are intimations of Thy greatness that no power can erase.

Into the fabric and fiber of my day are woven blessings that are greater than my mind can encompass. My soul overflows with joy at the multitude of Thy kindnesses to me.

Sustenance has been given in the perplexing day.
Patience has been given in the harried day.
Wisdom has been given in the needy day.
Fortitude has come in the weak moment.
Guidance has come in the confusing moment.
Comfort has come in the saddened moment.

Over and over Thy blessings appear, alive with the Holy, replete with the practical. May my day reverberate the praise my soul cannot hold back to Thee, Father, Son, and Abiding Spirit. Amen.

Midday

Save me this day, my God, from presuming on holy ground by underrating the invisible, overrating the tangible and ignoring the transcendent. Allow me to find out experientially what Jesus meant by feeding the poor, clothing the needy, visiting the prisoner, going the second mile, giving up anything that stands between me and love of God, forgiving seventy times seven. Then may I know Thy joy. Amen.

Evening

Judge of Life, have I been guilty of lapsing devotion, jealous thoughts, borrowed courage, lukewarm concern and anemic faith? Have I given a tart response, a curt reply, or scathing criticism? Have I been glib or devious or pretentious in any way? Would tenseness or bitterness or laziness describe my behavior? Have my attitudes been extreme? Have my actions been cavalier? Have I collaborated to defame, contemplated revenge, and ignored restitution? Have I been foolish and petty and blind?

O Lord, cleanse my heart so I may not hold any attitudes that serve to harm others and deny Thee. Replace every evil intent with caring grace.

How easily does wickedness of heart come to me. How often I have failed Christ when He needed me most. How often I have shut Christ out when He wanted in. How often I have denied Christ when He could have guided. How often I have turned from Christ when He was there, ready to meet me in my distress. Let me not fail Christ again. Let me not leave Christ hanging on the tree because I was blind and deaf and unrepentant.

Lord God, reveal to me as much of Thy will as I can assimilate. I would see Jesus. I would be Jesus' disciple. I would be saved. I would walk in this world with the mark of His Cross in my heart and the compassion of His love in my eyes. Amen.

Morning

Creator God, the beauty of the earth surrounds me. The sun has risen to reveal an abundance of flowers and trees, insects and animals, in size, shape, proportion, and variety beyond my imagination. l look at the green earth, the blue sky, the shadows sunlight casts on hill and valley and my heart is quickened to praise. I turn to catch a leaf whose pattern is so intricate that I marvel at the individuality and complexity in every corner of the universe.

My voice rises in gratitude:
> for sunrise nudging dawn aside;
> for rainfall landing in a trillion splashes;
> for symphonies of music from one mockingbird;
> for red roses in full summertime salute;
> for grey clouds tossed like pillows on a favorite couch;
> for white sycamores sharing autumn fragrance in an all night rain;
> for all shaking parts of happy puppies;
> for the glad chores of nectar-laden bumble bees;
> for the continual enthusiasm of scampering squirrels.

Were it not for this bounty of earth, my life would be impoverished. I glory all the more, that I know The Creator behind creation and ask that as I continue through this day my eyes would be opened to new revelations and my heart would find new avenues of praise for these daily benedictions. In The Name of The Lord Jesus Christ. Amen.

Midday

Let not the problems of this day overwhelm me, Lord. Give me to know Thy grace that is equal to all I may face now and reliable for eternity. Grant me perspective in perplexity, patience in trial, and strength in adversity. Through The Prince of Peace. Amen.

Evening

> Evening quiet
> Silent prayer
> Lord most Holy
> Thou art here.

God of might and glory
Whose origin is Thine own,
Whose ways are perfect,
Whose righteousness is above reproach,
Whose might is wrapped in mystery, whose love is em-
   bodied in Christ Jesus;
Let me listen for Thy call:

> Am I called to risk
>   but cling to the familiar?

> Am I called to trust
>   but become too anxious?

> Am I called to stewardship
>   but feign responsibility?

> Am I called to simplicity
>   but shun modesty?

> Am I called to prayer
>   but stay too busy?

> Am I called to sacrifice
>   but locked into acquisition?

In the night when Thy call is clearer, here in the
still moments when Thy quiet Presence is realized, help
me to evaluate my calling. My place in the world is
important to Thee. I would use my influence and relationships to honor Thee. Bless me, therefore, in my endeavors and guide me in the way everlasting.

> Pregnant silence
> Adoration,
> Accept O Lord,
> My meditation.
> Amen.

Summer

Summer has thoughts of its own; mature, rich, full-orbed with hindsight and possessed with wisdom. "Look how the year began," it seems to say, "and the privilege of what lies ahead." Summer knows when it has reached its peak and wants to take a while and bask in the finest it has to offer. Rather like a healing salve these sunset evenings with their lazy strolls into twilight; moments when the human soul is drawn to contemplate the Creator in a vesper of quiet meditation. Summer was made for the likes of us who need to pause and embrace a diversion from our usual pace; a favorite hideaway, alone or with friends, resting in our favorite way, noticing once again the warm relaxedness of the earth. Summers are for shaping memories, the magnificence of tree and flowers, seashore and mountain, sunshine and rain, the Good Lord still closing up shop for the night in the same colorful way and hanging the stars out to shine along the same lines.

God is not so far from us in summer. Those who find Him in Spirit and in truth correlate evidences of His handiwork in nature. One proceeds from the other; rainbows speak of a long kept vow, harvests speak of long promised blessings. In summer, The Christ of Judea, with His choice collection of rural illustrations comes easily to mind. We are not long on this earth before we too marvel at the potential of a mustard seed or of a grain of wheat dropped in the ground, or the singular beauty of a lily. The way Jesus couched His parables and performed his deeds was geared to open the human heart to greater trust. How like Him to pause in the summer wind, glance at the vines plump with grapes and the fields gold with wheat, and talk of faith.

We pause in summer, at the zenith of nature's munificent glory, and pray. We pray for greater belief in the purpose of the God we have come to know so intimately through our Lord, Jesus Christ. In such times the blessings of the good earth merge with growing faith into a benediction of grace.

Morning

Gracious God,
Who art the Source and Object of my praise,
Who encompasseth my days with blessings
Like the waters that cover the sea;
I recall the days of Jesus' earthly ministry
When He gave from strength
To all who came in weakness:

> To the blind He gave sight, to the sighted vision.
> To the fallen He granted forgiveness, to the forgiven
> renewal.
> To the tempted He gave strength, to the strong
> patience.
> To the needy He showed compassion, to the compas-
> sionate courage.
> To the hypocrites He gave warnings, to the humble
> righteousness.
> To the doubters He gave hope, to believers revelation.

Allow me to recognize as Jesus did:

> Cries beneath smiles, avoidance beneath activity;
> Escape beneath busyness, projection beneath
> accusation;
> Depression beneath pretense, insecurity beneath
> noise;
> Jealousy beneath praise, fear beneath silence;
> Rigidity beneath regulations, deceit beneath
> tenseness;

By Christ's power bring:

> Mistakes to forgiveness, ignorance to learning;
> Insecurity to maturity, fear to faith;
> Depression to insight, escapism to reality;
> Inferiority to wholeness, deceit to honesty;
> Rigidity to flexibility, faultfinding to self-worth.

I recall again how Jesus saw persons as they were and
encouraged the finest that was in them. Help me also to
catch the fervor of His belief in others and prioritize my
life around the truths He nourished then and nourishes
now.

> And may I believe with all my heart. Amen.

Midday

For those today who need me, crucially or informally,
For those today who teach me, positively or unknowingly,
For those today who touch me, physically or spiritually,
For those today who affirm me, verbally or non-verbally,
I express my gratitude, O Lord.
May I return with propriety what I receive in sincerity
And share in generosity what I know through the charity
Of faith in The Son. Amen.

Evening

Holy God,
Too near to touch,
Too mighty to deny,
Too mysterious to comprehend,
Unapproachable Awe yet knowable in love;
Accept my praise of Thee
    for Thy grace is more wonderful than I had known,
    Thy love is deeper than I can grasp,
    Thou art greater than all my dreams.
My heart shouts with praise for Thy faithfulness and
compassion. Thy protection has encompassed me all
through the day and attends me as I come to rest.

    May my unconscious mind, active while I am
asleep, feed on Thy precepts and be informed by Thy
scriptural counsel. Influence me, Father, in those areas of
my mind where I am least aware and where in sleep the
unacceptable and unthinkable are possible, for I commit
them to Thee also. Stabilize me with healthy mental
balance. In those realms of the mind where I am not
always aware and much is determined of which I am
never totally cognizant: inform, enlighten, direct, and
instruct, as pleases Thee.

    Thy Spirit, unbound and free, has led this heart
to its Creator. May that same Holy Spirit so pervade my
unconscious mind tonight that meshed with my conscious
desire to do Thy will, I may upon awakening, rise with
gratitude for a night of rest and praise for the joy of a new
day. To Thee, Holy God, who never slumbers nor sleeps,
all glory and honor in all aspects of this life and the life to
come. In Jesus' Name. Amen.

Morning

God, most merciful and understanding, who hath never failed me; whose Word is true, reliable and changeless; whose wisdom establishes justice in the earth; hear me as I confess these sins that grieve me and keep me from a full devotion to Thee:

half trust,
conditioned love,
unbridled words,
malicious thoughts,
undisciplined habits,
hasty conclusions,
reticent compassion,
unguarded criticism,
unrepented greed,
wavering faith,
evil deeds.

Allow that I may give full attention to these sins that warp my character and prevent the full light of Thy love to flow through me. I would be conformed to the image of The Living Christ, so alter, purge, sanctify, and build me according to Thy Holy Will.

Replace envy and strife with mercy and goodwill.
Replace uncleanness and impurity with holiness and restraint.
Replace malice and vindictiveness with forgiveness and restitution.
Replace fluctuation and faithlessness with steadiness and trust.

Allow me to be more like Jesus through whom I confess my sins and move on to greater trust. Amen.

Midday

Father, instill in me a rugged faith
Which no lesser allure can vanquish.
Let the motives of a pure heart,
The will of a loyal allegiance, and
The ideals of The Master,
Purify, pervade, and punctuate my desires.

Permit me to witness authentically and serve loyally
Where sorrow, shame, and pain,
Mar and hurt and maim,
That others may answer Jesus' claim
Yield their lives and praise His Name. Amen.

Evening

Almighty God, whose Face is veiled, whose majesty is robed in mystery, whose ways are awesome and mighty; sensitize me to the ways of spiritual maturity. Make me cognizant of the way biblical truth addresses everyday events and waits to be found and faithed. Reveal Life to me as "search" into silence, into suffering, into self, into knowledge, into relationships, into truth, into prayer, with Holy Spirit in it all.

Hear my gratitude for the sunshine of Thy blessings in the shadows of my search:

in the long stretches of silence, clues to Thy purposes emerged;

in the trying sieges of temptation, understandings of deliverance came;

in the long seasons of suffering, glimpses of Thy undergirding came;

in the long nights of grief, signs of Thy Presence appeared;

in the long days of struggle, signals of Thy grace were felt;

in the search for personhood scriptural truth affirmed;

in the valley of death's shadow, images of Thy glory shone.

God, Most Holy, lead me to act on the faith I have been given today and trust in humble obedience for the faith I will need tomorrow. Through The Christ of The Ages. Amen.

Morning

Illuminating Lord, whose Word is instruction, whose activity is love, whose promises are sure, open me to the opportunities and possibilities of this day.

Encourage me to stretch my soul, cherish the life of The Spirit, and be found often in prayer.

Lead me to do my work, not resentfully, but gratefully and faithfully.

Bring me to new ways of giving, sharing any gifts of personality and talent for the aid of others.

Challenge me to openness of mind, deeper learning, mind-stretching study, and clearer thought.

Encourage me to go outside my frame of reference to apply the ethics of Christ Jesus in a pluralistic and complex society.

Deepen me in relationships where concern is needed, friendship blossoms and sharing enhances.

Stir me out of laziness, indifference, and apathy concerning world peace.

Challenge me by the example of Christ, so His Words may be written in my heart and seen in my life.

Let me partake of the riches of this day with a grateful heart. May any failures in the past not curtail the promises of today. May I be as sensitive to spiritual realities as human need and make time to pray. If by word I can encourage or deed uplift; if by action I can bless or comment cheer; if by prayer I can undergird or letter affirm; allow me no hesitation in so doing with Christlike love. Amen.

Midday

Let courage be mine to bear this day what disappointment or burden began the day. Let me not be so imbalanced by circumstances as to deprive faith its chance. Let me not be so angry as to fail to forgive, so perplexed as to fail to pray, so discouraged as to give in to my weaker moments. All day long may I be imbued with the sound intelligence and straight thinking that fires faith, enriches relationships, confronts difficulty, and prods hope, through The Crucified and Risen Lord. Amen.

Evening

Father in heaven, Creator of all that is, forever concerned with all Thy children; I am drawn in evening reflection to recall my family, the home where I grew up, the home where I now live. I am grateful for the gifts of self-awareness and Christian piety that merged in the formative years. Allow me to pass to another generation those lessons from which I have benefited.

Be close to families where a parent is sick or missing and bills go unpaid.

Be close to families where a child lies handicapped or dying and sadness pervades the house.

Confront families where anger ravages uncontrolled, tainting minds and injuring bodies.

Strengthen families where the crucial years of forming sexual identity and learning fundamental trust arrive and parents struggle to spend quality time with their children.

Be close to families who are always in crises, where confused communication and emotional instability lead to hatred, jealousy, feuding, depression, and everyone seems to lose.

Be close to families with surrogate parents; fill them with an extra measure of Thy love.

Gracious Father, guard and keep my loved ones tonight. May those gathered under this roof forgive each other when they are wrong and affirm each other, as only families can, when they have achieved. Lead us to be reality oriented, to evaluate our motives in a context in keeping with Thy will. In all our gifts and diversity, agreements and disagreements, strengths and weaknesses, cohese our loyalty around Thy matchless love. In daily circumstance and family sharing lead us to maturity until one day we are joined with Thy Family in glory above. Through Christ, our Lord. Amen.

Morning

Holy God, Thou art a Great God and alone art worthy of my confession and obedience. Thou hast led me from darkness into light. Grant this day that the words of my mouth, the intent of my heart and the example of my actions might point to Christ, The Light of the World.

I am reminded of those:
who have light and use it,
who need light and can't find it,
who avoid light and despise it,
who require light and are ignorant of it,
who radiate light and share it,
who walk in the light and are directed by it.

Because all that is done in secret will be known openly,
Because we reap as we sow,
Because light is greater than darkness,
Prevent me from needing darkness to express myself
or preferring shadows to sunlight.

Allow that Thy Light may shine through me unhindered. May the radiance of The Master not be found wanting in my heart or dimmed in my eyes. As Thou hast led me in the past, lead me in the present and open me to the future, illumined from within, directed from without, enlightened from above.

O Thou Uncreated Light, in whom is no darkness nor shadow of turning, through whom all things were made that were made, in whom is my heart's desire and my soul's allegiance; I exalt and magnify Thy Holy Name, through The Son of Light. Amen.

Midday

Father of love,
Grant me a pure heart and a clear vision
To serve with compassion and care with mercy;
A clear mind and a stalwart will
To think deeply and act wholeheartedly;
A generous spirit and a humble attitude
To share unstintingly and with anonymity;
A loving approach and a committed purpose
To live victoriously and in joy. Amen.

Evening

Holy God, I reflect in the quiet of the night on the busy hours of the day:

Have I failed to hear a muted cry for acceptance?

Have I missed a veiled cry for help?

Have I ignored a sincere plea for justice?

Have I been so involved in my own life that I was unable to relate to the struggle of another?

Have I lived less than I intended by settling for less than was possible?

It is not always easy for me to catch myself, Father, overextending, going for goals and missing persons, looking for rewards and overlooking needs. May my eyes be drawn to Jesus who was never imbalanced by the pressures of life and used the simple things of the earth to pinpoint the profound: grain, bread, seeds, coins, fish, trees. May the pattern of my intentions be more in keeping with The Master's example. Center me on life's essentials and shape me in Love's service according to Thy will. Amen.

Morning

Holy God, may I not use today amiss. In the light of Thy boundless love and amazing grace, let me put these hours to good use. Fill me with acuity of thought and surety of action that bring praise to Thy Name. If my hands get dirty, so be it. If my body grows weary, so be it. If my mind and spirit are taxed to the full, so be it. Let me not leave this world as I found it. Let wickedness be bravely faced and evil courageously challenged. Let my noblest feelings be expressed in representing Thy love in the world's neediest places. Let faith be increased and mercy spread abroad.

I am purposeless and rootless without Thee. I would wander the earth aimless and visionless were it not for Thy Revelation. How can it be that I have ever known Thee, ever sought Thy counsel and found therein the Words of Life? I marvel at Thy goodness to me and at the profundity and depth with which my struggles are addressed and met. To know Thee is to want to know Thee more, to want to plunge to the deep recesses of redemptive purpose for human life. To commune with Thee is to be caught up in Thy purposes for this world and to be led into service for Thy Kingdom. Lead me now, O Lord, lead me still. Amen.

Midday

How often I have prayed Father, despondent, dejected, and harried by the pace of life, only to find in praying new strength for the task, new perspective on problems, and renewed hope for the future. Implant in me The Spirit of Christ, who was equal to every occasion, faithful in every circumstance and loyal to the Father's will, even death on a cross. Amen.

Evening

Merciful God, slow to anger, quick to forgive, plenteous in mercy, generous in pardon, whose justice is sure and judgment perfect; I question my motives:

Have I concealed facts to distort truth and get my own way?

Have I overreacted to what I oppose because of my secret attraction?

Have I covered up so long that I no longer delineate deception from the truth?

Have I avoided confessing my faults to one other because I am spiritually lax?

Have I denied love to promote pleasure and reaped emptiness?

Have I underrated the perceptivity of Jesus to perpetuate my viewpoint?

Have I lived ignorant of the Scriptures because I would not study their meaning?

Have I failed to speak to others of my faith in Christ Jesus because I have so little faith to share?

Have I avoided prayer because I knew there was something I needed to do, or something I needed to be rid of?

Have I ever tried to bless others as I have been blessed?

Forgive me where I have lowered my standards with mixed motives and weak resolve. Merge trust with obedience in Thy forgiving pardon. Give me courage to rectify and power to overcome. For Jesus' sake. Amen.

Morning

Eternal God,
Who art more willing to give than I am to ask,
Deliver me this day from all lethargy and laziness
That separates me from the task at hand.
Energize me to do that which I have to do
And to avoid doing that which can only divide me.

In this day may I be:
> kind to the thoughtless,
> patient with the rude,
> attentive to the needy,
> appropriate with the demanding,
> sympathetic with the suffering,
> firm with the manipulative,
> compassionate with the broken,
> wise with family,
> fair with self,
> loyal to Christ.

I praise Thee for every reflection of Thy Presence
That shines back at me in the eyes of others,
That brings comfort in dire straits,
And steady light on dark days.
Center my life in trust of Thee and
Express Thy life through me today
In Jesus' Holy Name. Amen.

Midday

God of Providence,
May I this day be more cheerful.
Let me express joy for my blessings,
Gratitude for my challenges and
Praise for my privileges.
Restrain me from discouragement
That does not fit the facts.
Let me not be dour and dejected and afraid.
Stabilize me in the reality of faith's courage,
With the blessings of love's service
Through the power of The Holy Spirit. Amen.

Evening

O Loving Father, I cannot lie down to sleep tonight without thinking of those with problems greater than mine. In Thee is my hope; may those for whom I pray find their hope in Thee also.

I pray for those who wander, drifting aimlessly,
 Seeking what they cannot find,
 Finding what they do not need,
 Using what uses them and not caring.
Bring them to repentence and faith.

I pray for those who forage among the hopes of the past,
 Finding the present unsuitable,
 Looking for times that never were,
 Building a future that can never be.
Bring them to themselves.

I pray for those who are lonely and ache inside,
 Mourning the loss of a loved one,
 Recalling those arms that held them,
 Remembering that voice and manner.
Open them to others.

I pray for those who run from responsibility,
 Preferring childishness to maturity,
 Mocking the moral order,
 Trying relationships and credulity to the full.
Realign them with reality.

I pray for those who run from responsibility,
 Preferring childishness to maturity,
 Mocking the moral order,
 Trying relationships and credulity to the full.
Realign them with reality.

Holy God, lift all this night who in any way need Thy redeeming power and seal their salvation in The Savior through The Spirit that watches us all. Amen.

Morning

Lord of yesterday and tomorrow, who of the past has been faithful; of the present, my Guide; of the future my Sure Hope; allow me to see and act today, in ways appropriate to the needs of those I meet. There are those:

who are always in conflict,
who let events embitter them,
who do not believe in themselves,
who masquerade happiness,
who are imbalanced by life's demands,
who mock religion,
who cannot keep up images anymore,
who want nothing to do with God.

These persons cross my path and my consciousness daily. I can visualize them in their need, continuing to prolong their self-defeating ways. Give me also to visualize Thy Presence making a difference in them. Perhaps this will be mediated through me or through another. I pray for a deft hand and an educated heart to know those ways best suited to meet their needs. As events come to pass, may the urgings of The Holy Spirit illumine, convict, and bring them to salvation.

O Father of Mercies, how could I have known Thee, found Thee, loved Thee without the nurture and assistance of others? My prayer rises in gratitude for them, for the Word by which we are led and instructed; for the Spirit by whom we are convicted and guided; for The Son in whom we are saved and sanctified, now and always. Is there not some way in word and deed that I may express these joys today to another? In The Savior's Love. Amen.

Midday

May I use these hours wisely, O Lord, as a servant who numbers his days unto wisdom. May I not waste precious moments on minor concerns or petty diversions. Free me to a flexibility that garners understanding and utilizes trust. Let my values in time be informed by Thy precepts from beyond time. May my faith in Christ Jesus lead me to appropriate present challenges for eternal possibilities through The Spirit's Guidance. Amen.

Evening

Eternal God, my Fortress and Salvation; I am reminded of the flow of events which seemed unrelated at the time, yet merged into a benediction that has risen to bless my life.

Through gratitude I am deepened and enlarged:
    for times of silent meditation that made the difference,
    for moments of communion that pinpointed options,
    for hours of comfort when peace could not be shaken;
    for minutes of struggle in a Gethsemane of prayer,
      where Spirit held precedence over flesh;
    for temptations conquered;
    for suffering shared;
    for love triumphant over hate;
    for joy that outlasts sorrow;
    for peace that cannot be destroyed.

How often Thy deliverance has come to me and I have not been thankful. Praise and gratitude fill my heart for Thy great gift in Christ Jesus. Previously I had been immersed in self concerns, in envy, pride, and lost endeavors. Then I was brought to conviction of my sin and bathed in the blood of Thy Lamb. My transgressions were blotted out; my sins covered. Thy cleansing has erased the stains of the past and I am free to walk in newness of life.

      God above me,
      God beside me,
      God within me,
      God of Love;

I praise Thee forever, through Jesus, my Savior. Hallelujah. Amen.

Morning

God of Wisdom and Mercy, I dedicate my life to Thee this day. Were I to meet one with a need I could answer, I pray I would. Were I to meet the unexpected and be a resource for referral, I pray I might. Were I called to make a sacrifice of time or money, I pray I would be willing. In all these matters I pray to be motivated by Christ Jesus, who lived His earthly days in love made perfect through obedience to the will of The Father.

All around me I see:
> the rigidity of the perfectionists,
> the dourness of the lazy,
> the tartness of the rude,
> the tenseness of the worried,
> the inertia of the lazy,
> the sham of the insincere,
> the counterproductiveness of the bitter,
> the hardness of the jealous,
> the fatigue of the faithless.

I am reminded of those qualities in myself. Join me with
> the joy of the benevolent,
> the health of the forgiving,
> the insight of the thoughtful,
> the optimism of the faithful,
> the productiveness of the generous,
> the genuineness of the kind,
> the dreams of the visionary,
> the persistence of the patient,
> the hopefulness of the prayerful.

Lead me from weakness to strength, from immaturity to maturity, from concern to action, from simple trust to greater faith. Through Christ Jesus, my Lord. Amen.

Midday

Father of all good gifts, whose gift of life in Thy only begotten Son, Jesus, outshines all other gifts; accept my noontime praise for the redemption whereby I am saved:
> for the efficacy and price of it;
> for the security and surety of it;
> for the individuality and totality of it;
> for the message it entails and the gospel it proclaims;
> for the life it evokes and the love it bestows.

May even my unguarded moments reflect the salvation I
know in my prayerful moments. Through the
Redeemer's Power. Amen.

Evening

Blessed Lord, the life of The Spirit is so rich and
deep, living by faith so adventurous and hopeful, that
this night I pause to recount those blessings the realized
Presence of Christ has given me to know:
the guidance of Scripture,
promises of hope,
the cleansing of confession,
forgiveness from sin,
well springs of joy,
strength in temptation,
the power of worship,
a desire for God,
indifference to possessions,
a mind at peace,
realistic self-esteem,
insight into godliness,
the wooing of Holy Spirit,
redeeming love.

How can it be, though unaware, a desire for God
has come to me? How can it be, though undeserving,
grace has found me? How can it be, though rebellious,
my heart has found its peace in God?

Increase in me all that cries out for Thee:
lest I harden myself to truth, pursue false gods and
reap in shame;
lest I ignore others, shun need and increase pain;
lest I yield to sin, ignore Scripture and stifle allegiance;
lest I falter on my promises, deny my commitments
and dishonor Christ.

I give my life into Thy keeping tonight. Let my
heart be in Thy control and my mind set on Thy will. Let
those whom I love and those who call to Thee in distress
be equally surrounded by Thy grace. Sustain me in Thy
care and in whatever tomorrow brings, may the prayers
of this day prepare me for the challenges of those moments. Through The Incarnate Son. Amen.

Morning

In spite of Thy patience, O Lord, I often look around and find I have reversed my priorities, prayed one way and lived another. Often I have:

needed deliverance but would not leave the vicinity of temptation;

requested joy and was unwilling to humble myself in selfless service;

desired peace of mind and missed the peace of God;

needed courage and withdrew from the struggle before the challenge was over;

desired wealth and did not understand the rate of exchange in God's sight;

sought acceptance but did not meet others halfway;

wanted the gifts of God but purchased the trinkets of earth.

Can it be Thou doest stand at my heart's door, knocking, and I do not answer? Can it be that I make up my mind first about what is best for me, and only seek later the counsel of Scripture? Do I ask for that which plainly contradicts Thy purposes to fulfill my own desires?

I pray, Lord, for Thy centering will. May I learn the obedience of a faithful follower who takes time to listen in prayer and remains sensitive to the leadership of the Holy Spirit, who with Thee and The Son, reigns in glory forever. Amen.

Midday

A sinner lost
Thy love embraced.
Saved my soul,
My life then graced
With hope and trust,
Joy unfolding:
God of glory,
I adore Thee.

Evening

Loving God, the beauty of a summer evening is
all about me, the warmth, the aliveness of the night, the
wafting of gentle breezes, the wide and open sky. In this
time of reverie and slackened pace, I pause to take
measure of my life:

Have I been as available to my family as I ought to be?
Have I been honest and loyal in my business?
Have I been as an equal to my mate?
Have I given freely?
Have I deepened friendship with authenticity?
Have I settled for mediocrity?
Have I been faithful in studying the Scriptures?
Have I grown more patient?
Have I majored on possessions to the exclusion of
relationships?
Have I supported right as I knew it?
Have I prayed for my enemies?

Holy Spirit, as I emerge from this self-examination,
build in my heart the resolve to improve in those areas
where my life is lacking and lead me to others and lead
others to me to accomplish Thy holy will. Amen.

Morning

Holy Father, in Thee is my completeness, my wholeness, my health. Thou hast kept me through a night of rest and wakened me to a day of opportunity. I am grateful that as I have need of Thee, Thou hast the power to fill the need and even now my strength is being renewed so I may walk with steady step into the demands of this day.

Let my gratitude go deeper than need, for I am grateful that before I knew how to respond to Thee, Thou didst care for me, Thou didst plan my life and long for my redemption. I am thankful for that spark within me which first caused me to desire Thee, to repent my sinful ways and let Jesus Christ into my heart.

Let no sin hold me from confessing.
Let no hurt hold me from forgiving.
Let no reversal halt my best intentions.
Let no criticism warp my spirit.
Let no disappointment make me bitter.
Let no failure find me hiding.
Let no circumstance keep me from prayer.

May this day be one of spiritual growth, of faithful obedience and renewed trust through Christ Jesus, who sanctified life and made crucifixion a sacrament of grace. Amen.

Midday

Sovereign God,
I remember those for whom this day is confusing.
They walk but do not arrive,
They search but do not find,
They ask and do not hear,
They knock and find no response,
Because they do not know how to receive.
Thou hast so much for us, Generous Lord,
If we are open enough to receive it.
Make me bold to accept what faith trusts and hope believes
Through the confidence Love brings. Amen.

Evening

Gracious and Merciful Father,
I contemplate this evening, the life of Christ,
Perfect and faithful in every respect,
Worthy of my highest praise and life's allegiance:

I remember the personality of Jesus:
    His winsomness and approachability,
    His candor and unobstructed gaze,
    His acuity of mind and refreshing wit,
    His patience and simplicity,
    His authority and courage.
As I contemplate the character of Jesus
May I be conformed to His image.
May His attitudes be reflected in my own, through:
  His power in prayer,
    His matchless teachings,
      His concern for justice,
        His strong leadership,
          His notice of the rejected,
            His way with children,
              His respect for women,
                His righteous anger,
                  His selfless sharing,
                    His trust in God,
                      His uncomplaining death.
  Though never wrong, He wronged no one.
  Though never unfaithful, He believed in others.
  Though never unkind, He loved the unkind.

      I recall how Jesus, innocent of false charges,
submitted to unprecedented injustice to win salvation for
all. Through His obedience evil was robbed of its sting
and flesh was robed in Redemption. Center my affections
around the cross-borne reality of the Risen Christ, who
lives and reigns with Thee and the Spirit, here and
hereafter, world without end. Amen.

Morning

Omnipotent God, the fury and pain and death of the world are before me. Hunger and war curse the landscape of the earth, wasting lives that barely had a chance, lives that fell victim to forces greater than preventive measures could halt. Thus does the world groan and travail. The people of the earth are displaced, disenchanted, disenfranchised, disillusioned. Will the cheating, hatred, and depersonalization never cease? Lives are maimed, cornered, confused, misused, and left to die on lonely roads at the end of shattered dreams. Day and night the prayers of the broken rise to Thee; day and night the prayers of the faithful join in chorus for the deliverance of the suffering. Wilt Thou raise up brave women and men to prophesy and proclaim sure judgment against the forces of evil that would trample human dignity and curtail human freedom? Let justice rise up in the earth and peace surround the nations of the world.

Let me not think to walk among the cries of the starving, the pleas of the poor, the pain of the homeless, and live indifferently. Forgive all such tendencies in me. If I need to fast to fight hunger, if I need to get involved to bring peace, if I need to take a towel and kneel at the feet of the suffering to bring the message of Hope from a God of love, then so discipline me, so motivate me, so kneel me beneath the cross of Jesus that I may toil in the center of the world's pain and at last, see heaven's light. Amen.

Midday

Let what I have done since this day began and what I do until its close be pleasing in Thy sight, O Lord. By relinquishment of pride and compassion for others, may I paint from the pigments of each hour a painting sensitive in service, resilient in spirit, and glowing with the light of Divine Love. Amen.

Evening

Almighty God, in whom alone I live and breathe, and trust for things in heaven and earth; my thoughts are of Thee as darkness comes. Thou hast sustained me through the day and art my dwelling place at night.

In a world where the flamboyant and spectacular easily attract attention, I offer a prayer of gratitude for:

the simplicity of a bowl of apples,
the sparkle in the eyes of happy children,
the smile of a loving older parent,
the shades of orange in a sunset,
the moving strength of fine portraits,
the tenderness of a loving touch,
the blue morning glories circling an old mailbox,
the singular beauty of a flowering peach tree,
the delightful magic of first winter snowfall,
the variegated colors of butterfly wings,
the sacred symbolism of a piece of bread,
a cup of wine: "in remembrance" . . . till He come.

Allow me to appreciate the way profundity and richness are often wrapped in simplicity, Lord, and wrap my life in the deep truths of The Master who said, "I am the way, the truth, and the life." Amen.

Morning

Let me keep silence before Thee, Great God, and not require the verbal as the only means of communication. Let my prayer ascend into the mystery of Thyself and fill my soul with the beauty of Thy Presence. Shake me from the belief that holds to only certain patterns and forgets the Creator who threw the molds away. As I contemplate Thy goodness, Thy Creative energy, Thy Omnipotent power, may I be awed anew with the power of a God who could surround Himself with a universe and not be covered, who could people a planet and not be unaware of a bird's fall, who could send an only begotten Son to save a sinful people and not forever be impoverished. Where else can my soul find repose but in Thee? Thy ways are past finding out and Thy greatness is unapproachable.

Know me, Father. Search me. Direct me. Let my steps be honorable in Thy sight and my words shaped by the meaning of Thy silence. I pray through Him who spoke and still speaks, who lived and still lives, who interceded and still intercedes: The Lamb slain before the foundation of the earth: Christ Jesus. Amen.

Midday

Loving Lord,
For faith revised and vision increased,
For hope renewed and trust released,
For love rekindled and hope fulfilled,
I sing Thy praise and seek Thy will.
Amen.

Evening

Creator God, like mercy Thy Light falls when needed most, highlighting new alternatives when the mind is weary and the heart is sad, illuminating old Scriptures when the soul is needy and the countenance drops.

How like Thy grace the sun is, shining in lonely hearts, warming discouraged hearts, brightening saddened hearts, showing new paths, blessing all who choose its blessings, shining freely and without cost.

The sun that opened flower and leaf in spring has brought them to their peak: bloom gives way to fruit, leaflets to branches, acorn to tree.

> For the interplay of sunlight and shadow;
> for places of brightness near bowers of shade;
> for forests of green near lakes of blue;
> for fields of grain near wild growing flowers;

I give praise today. Without sunlight, moonlight would have no contrast, earth would dry up, dark night would overwhelm. Without the Light of The World, my soul would languish in the darkness of sin. I would find no victory. I could know no peace. Yet, in the face of Christ Jesus, a great Light shines. Now sin is ultimately defeated. Salvation shines in the hearts of believers. Illumine my soul in Thy beauty until I am enveloped in the glow of heaven around Thy mighty throne. Amen.

Autumn

Autumn, like all the seasons, begins a little earlier than one suspects. The wild grasses and weeds brown out and appear to be curling up for the winter. They pass the word along, before frost appears, then aging goldenrod and thistle join the masquerade. Mullen, hollyhock, and stalks of corn stand tanning, browned, given over to last things. Slowly the leaves of artistic trees give new definition to orange and scarlet. Some trees drop acorns from their gold-lined branches and the ever deft squirrels, wild with excitement, run to bury their winter store or pause on a high limb with curled up tail to eat in joyous abandon.

Autumn is alive with coppery colors dancing in the sunlight. Red reveals more shadings than we knew before from watermelon pink to the deep maroon of the shiny oak leaf. Yellow pales to a rich cream on the gourd and the orange that dresses pumpkins seems irridescent in the sun-drenched glow of the sugar maple.

In the clarity of harvest moon the perfect formation of geese winging their way South can be seen; the night air is cold and old October braces for a wintry blast.

Harvest comes with a magnificent bounty. Thankfulness can be riveted in the mind by contemplating what life would be like if the crops failed, if the rains did not come, if devastation covered the land. It is hard to imagine, yet we who pray realize there are those who suffer the ravages of malnutrition because they have never had enough to eat.

In autumn when the bright earth is blessed with the fruits of the land, Jesus, who reveals The Father perfectly, comes to the praying heart, quietly, thoughtfully, and asks as He always has asked, always is asking, always will ask: "Do you love me?" "Have you fed my sheep?" And we who are so well fed must think of those who are not so well fed and obey this Master, who comes to us in so many ways, in so many seasons and places; yet never so urgently, I think, as in the need of others. "To whom much has been given" say the Scriptures, "much is required." The soul of autumn is the stewardship of harvest.

Morning

Almighty God,
Who hath given me this day;
The sight to see it and the insight to cope with it.
May I not be so prescribed by routine
Or driven by pressures
That I overlook the real struggles of others:

> Weakened by hunger or sidelined by disease,
> Hounded by mistakes or blinded by greed,
> Imbalanced by temptation or unnerved by worry,
> Cornered by depression or controlled by habit,
> Goaded by conscience or splintered by hate,
> Distraught by grief or swayed by impulse,
> Trapped by guilt or weakened by drink.

May I also not fail to see the cumulative effect of my
efforts in whatever direction I go. O Thou, who knowest
all about me and loves me still, sensitize me to an
awareness of others undergirded by Scripture and prayer
that will be efficacious, will in the process of relating and
sharing bear fruit honorable to Thy Name and The Lord
Jesus Christ whom this day I am called to serve. Amen.

Midday

Regnant Lord,

Still, still my troubled heart,
Renew my weary soul.
Reclothe me in my inward parts,
Restore and make me whole.

Tame, tame my restless will,
Chasten my wandering heart.
Convict me by Thy Holy Word,
Challenge and shed Thy Light.
Amen.

Evening

Grant me an open mind, O God, one not so tied to the past as to be unable to embrace the future. May I think deeply, studying and digging for truth. May I seek out the right questions before embracing the wrong answers. May I be flexible enough to change my mind when my mind needs changing and to expand my mind when the issues require re-evaluation.

When others share their hurts with me, let me be quiet and weigh my responses. Show me the philosophy behind their words, the principles or lack thereof behind their behavior, the emotions behind their adjectives, and the options that might free them.

Give me the wisdom to listen with an educated heart.
Save me from the folly of presuming and the sin of
    judging.
Save me from the dangers of despair and the uselessness
    of worry.
Let me not be torn from belief in others because others do
    not believe in themselves.
Let me not feel the compulsion to solve others' problems
    but undergird them as they find their own solutions.
Let me be kind for I seldom understand another's hurts.
Lead me to pray with others and for others because Thou
    hast designed us to find Thy will in mutual prayer.
Lead me to that spark of beauty found in all persons and
    deftly love it to fruition.

So be in my mind and in my heart that I may from day to day increase in wisdom and stature, as did Jesus, and in favor with Thee, O Lord, and those with whom Thou hast given me to live for Thy Name's sake. Amen.

Morning

God, Most Holy, as the day slows down and
crimson sunset catches suntanned hill and golden valley
in one last glow of autumn, so quiet and fill me with Thy
Spirit. Allow in that which I recall with joy, affirmation,
and that which I remember with regret, cleansing.

How often Thy Spirit led and I ventured not,
How often Thy mercy appeared and I knew it not.
How often Thy forgiveness fell and I appreciated not.
How often Thy glory shone and I saw not:
How often Thy chastisement came and I compre-
hended not.
How often Thy Word instructed and I followed not.
How often the still small Voice and I heard not.

Let me not be too busy, insensitive, or unaware
of Thy dealings with me. Open my eyes that I may see,
my ears that I may hear, my intuition that I may sense
and my mind that I may contemplate Thy greatness and
mercy. Open me to the Holy, hide me in Thy righteousness, undergird me with Thy forgiveness, and surround
me with Thy love. Through Christ Jesus, The Redeemer.
Amen.

Midday

The guidance faith brings,
The joy service brings,
The strength hope brings,
The resolution prayer brings,
The comfort Scripture brings,
The guidance Spirit brings:
These are the gifts my soul sings
In celebrative rememberings,
To Thee, O King of Kings,
Through whom I enjoy all things.
Amen.

Evening

God of Mercy,
When I glance beneath the surface of my all-too-hasty day,
I find motivations so suspect as to deny love a chance.
In thoughtless word and compulsive deed,
I have bartered the faith I claim and claimed behavior
That denied faith expression.

I know the ways of:
>a taunting temperament and reckless words,
>a resentful attitude and caustic comments,
>an uncaring outlook and benign indifference,
>a quick temper and hasty judgment,
>a closed mind and apathetic concern,
>anxious thoughts and presumptive worry.

Thou knowest how far my pride has carried me,
how shabby my witness, how impoverished my soul.
Forgive me for taking the clues for character from the
whim of the moment instead of The Christ of the ages.

If obedience falters, let discipline continue;
If trust wavers, let faith overcome;
If courage weakens, let hope endure;
If understanding fails, let mercy apply;
If sorrow comes, let the Spirit comfort;
If temptation lures, let commitment surmount.

Allow that in all circumstances I may be enabled
to do what is necessary, through Christ who strengthens me.
Let Christ be central, Christ pivotal, Christ, The Mediator,
who shapes me in service on earth for Thy glory above.
Amen.

Morning

O Light to all that seek and mercy to all that find;
forgive me for prayers:
> that hide more than they reveal,
> that ring only half true,
> that fail to take Thee seriously,
> that cover emergencies only,
> that fill up space and not heart,
> that pretend more than they are,
> that are overborne with emotion,
> that try to manipulate,
> that never stop to listen,
> that ignore mystery,
> that are imbalanced by demand,
> that falsify concern, underrate sin, and fall
> dangerously short of Thy will.

Lord, teach me to pray:
> if in praise I lack adoration;
> if in confessing I show no remorse;
> if in petition I show no faith;
> if in thanksgiving my heart is cold;
> if in invoking the Name of Jesus
> my will is not in it;

Purge me from my sin and lead me to a true confession.
Through the blood of The Everlasting Lamb. Amen.

Midday

> Gracious Lord,
> Who unwraps the darkness of the night
> With the brightness of the day;
> Remove from my life all dark and devious ways
> And fashion me in the glad light of faith
> That I may readily serve Thee
> In the joy and blessing of Christ, my King.
> Amen.

Evening

Protecting and Powerful God, I remember those facing
acute adjustment:

>who are moving to a nursing home tomorrow,
>who buried a loved one today,
>who are unemployed,
>who face a life sentence,
>who have been evicted,
>who went too far and stayed too long,
>who worshiped the wrong god,
>who are held on false charges,
>who trusted someone and lost most of their earnings,
>who know better and refuse to stop,
>who divorced for their protection,
>who are trapped by resentment.

Lord, be very close to those for whom life has not
turned out as they expected. Depression has momentarily
clouded faith and darkness surrounds them.

Is any anguish so deep Thou doest not understand?
Is any distance so far Thou canst not reach?
Is any shadow so dark Thou canst not see?
Is any hurt so great Thou canst not heal?

Join me tonight, with those who feed on Thy
Word and sit quietly in Thy Presence until the majesty
and availability of The Master pervades, even now, even
here, even in turmoil. Then commune with me in the
mystery, allow me to come to terms with the silence, bring
Thy promises to mind, gradually lead me to see Thy ways
and act on those glimpses of glory that will not go away. It
is enough. Amen.

Morning

Eternal God, my Fortress and Salvation, who never forsakes nor abandons, who is plenteous in mercy and generous in love, who hath not dealt with me unfairly and whose righteousness is worthy of all praise; on this new day I am reminded of the flow of events which seemed unrelated at the time, yet merged into a benediction that has risen to bless my life.

> The friend of a friend through whom I discovered new gifts in myself;
>
> The disappointment that led me to seek help and find more than what I sought;
>
> The cancellation that left open a new option and revealed a waiting truth;
>
> The relationship that taught me new levels of caring;
>
> The Scripture that fit an event in an unusual way and brought me closer to Thee;
>
> The call for help that taught me more than the person in need.

Through gratitude I am deepened and enlarged:

> There were times of silent meditation that made all the difference;
>
> There were moments of communion that pinpointed opportunities;
>
> There were hours of comfort when peace could not be shaken;
>
> There were minutes of struggle in a Gethsemane of prayer when Spirit held precedence over flesh.

Let me be sensitive to Thy working in my life. May I look beneath the surface and claim The Power that claims my soul. May I seek the gifts of The Spirit, as in Thy Providence I am sought. May my soul garner the promises that cannot be denied. May my heart ring with the joy of one who in prayer and service has sought God, desired God, and found God. Through faith in The Only Begotten of God. Amen.

Midday

Slow me down, Father, to a pace in keeping with Thy will instead of my frenzy. Allow me time to think, time to contemplate, time to pray. Then fill me in my rushed moments with the calm of my prayerful moments for my good and Thy glory. Amen.

Evening

Eternal God, my Heavenly Father, who hath given me all I possess and withheld nothing I need; can it be that I have walked by blazing but unconsumed bushes of need and failed to see? Can it be that I have crossed on dry land between raging seas of temptation and failed to be grateful for my deliverance? Have I missed the Light of God leading to those who are in pain, because I was attracted to the lights that so soon fade?

Indeed, I have eaten from the fruit of the tree in the center of the garden and become engrossed in my pride. Days pass and I miss the clues that the eyes of faith see so easily. Through neglect the attrition of my sin is upon me. The thoughtless word, the insensitive reaction, the imprudent criticism, the unjust remark, the needless attack have fallen from my lips, revealing a sin-covered heart.

Have I also:
> betrayed my highest hopes,
> severed my commitments,
> disregarded my beliefs,
> denied my resolves,
> neglected my duties,
> disdained my blessings and
> missed the joy of my Lord?

Loving Father, forgive my defection. I am sorry for my ingratitude and pride. As I confess, may I also be forgiven and live to serve The Savior who died to save me from my sin. Amen.

Morning

Lord of Life, Guardian and Guide of those that
seek Thee with a whole heart:

Let my spirit be subject to Thy will.
Let my actions match my commitment.
Let my words express a grateful heart.
Let my feet follow in straight paths.
Let my hands finish what they begin.
Let my body be controlled by Thy Spirit.
Let my eyes reflect The Inner Light.

Often I have:

prayed for Thy kingdom and avoided its work,
sought righteousness yet lived in unrighteousness,
requested strength yet denied its power,
received mercy yet failed to appropriate it,
pleaded forgiveness yet failed to forgive,
desired faith but clung to anxiety,
coveted freedom but rejected its responsibility,
wanted happiness and forgotten to share.

Let me not deny that which enriches nor ignore
that which strengthens. When Thou callest to me, may I
answer as a citizen of two worlds, serving obediently in
one with a watchful eye on the other. For all that draws
my wandering gaze from earth to heaven, from time to
eternity, from life's darkly hid vale to Thy Face fully
revealed, I praise Thee, Gracious Father, Loving Son,
Wooing Spirit. Amen.

Midday

Lord of Hosts,
Thy mercy bids me.
Thy Spirit moves me.
Thy compassion stirs me.
Thy love surrounds me.
Thy goodness enables me
To serve and adore Thee
Through Christ Jesus: Life to me.
Hallelujah, I praise Thee.
Amen.

Evening

Omnipotent and Omnipresent Lord,
Reign in my heart with patience and forgiveness.
Stay the judgment my hasty actions deserve:

Do I expect from others mercy I am unwilling to extend
    myself?
Do I condone in private what I approve in public?
Do I place the pursuit of pleasure above the seeking of
    Thy will?
Do I extend to some, compassion I would be unwilling to
    share with all?
Do I allow the body a generous appetite and starve the
    soul?
Do I see myself as more important than others with less?

Have I in carelessness polluted and expected cleanliness
    in return?
Have I avoided the mettle of meekness in order to prove
    my own strength?
Have I rated the plight of the hungry and destitute of less
    importance than they are to Thee?
Have I mocked decency, sneered at purity, and expected
    immunity from the venture?
Am I ungrateful for the simple blessings of each day?
Does the value I place on myself depend more on what I
    do than who I am?

Holy God, prioritize my life around the Faultless Life of
    Christ.
Foster discernment, bestow wisdom, extend mercy.
Inspire me not only to see but to act;
To portray in deed what I understand in fact
Through faith in The Son,
Who fused the two in perfect obedience. Amen.

Morning

God of Mystery and Holiness,
I rejoice in the opportunities of this day,
Moments in which to work, relate, relax, and pray.
May I not become so immersed in activities
That I forget the difficulties of others.

> I pray for those who never had an opportunity and
> are waiting;
> For those who had their opportunity and passed it
> by;
> For those who think opportunities mysteriously come
> to them instead of creating their own;
> For those who have made their opportunity and are
> using it to the full.

Allow those who know to do.
Teach those who have not known to learn.
Prod those who do not know they know to discover.
Encourage those who know enough to share.
Strengthen those who know and do to be generous with
their knowledge for the good of others.
Bless all, who through The Spirit's work, know Thee and
thus know, even as they are known, the love of God in
Christ Jesus. Amen.

Midday

O Thou alone, who knowest my heart
Yet ever worketh for my salvation,
Grant me this day,
>   grace to listen,
>   patience to wait,
>   wisdom to act and
>   strength to continue
In the will that centers and the hope that sustains through
  The Christ who saves. Amen.

Evening

Lord, most gracious, I recall the life of Christ, His joyful birth, His faultless life, the sufferings and death He endured, His triumphant Resurrection and glorious Ascension. I remember His willing conformity to Thy will, His strength in healing, His rightness in chastising, His penetrating insight, His unwavering love. May His way of life become more deeply engrained in mine for I have been guilty of:

> exchanging truth for half truth;
> swapping joy for pleasure;
> trading purity for broadmindedness;
> bartering loyalty for favors;
> entertaining deceit for gain.

When I think of Christ my failures become more vivid. I ask forgiveness for these sins, a chance to change, and a new opportunity to honor The Nazarene in word and deed. Amen.

Morning

God of Providence, I would want to live today better than yesterday—wiser, stronger, more aware, and better able to respond to others. In Thy Providence I have been planted in this place, among these people, given this task to do. Help me to accept and value my part in the scheme of things and be faithful even in little, sure that in Thy will much will come of it.

I pray a special blessing on those whom others often overlook because they blend into the background and are subject to indirect attention:

maids and custodians,
waiters and cashiers,
dishwashers and cooks,
street cleaners and window washers,
service station attendants and cab drivers,
assistants and associates,
orderlies and gardeners,
switchboard operators and messengers.

Let me not overlook those who grant services nor fail to speak a word of appreciation to them. Hear my thankfulness that in Thy grace none of Thy children are overlooked. Keep me seeing as Christ Jesus did, and caring with the care which He took for the unnoticed and unwanted. May I be faithful in service, for Thy Kingdom is built on the sacrificial lives of those who have been denied comfort to gain peace and who have relinquished glory of earth to gain reward of heaven.

With Thy unction fill me. With Thy compassion lead me. With Thy courage let me be found today, sharing with someone the kindness so generously lavished upon me. Through Jesus, my Lord. Amen.

Midday

Shepherd of this fragile life,
Whose pastures green and waters still
Feed my soul and life fulfill;
Whose mercy hallows every breath
Grace bestowing in life or death;
Closely hold me in Thy fold
Love to know and truth uphold;
Shepherd of eternal life.
Amen.

Evening

Father of Mercies and all comfort, I pause to examine my response to Thee. When Thou callest to me, am I preoccupied? Am I busy about other matters and unconcerned? Do I crave glory and honor so that self-interest comes before Kingdom concerns? Do I evaluate matters based on any inappropriate hunger for success? Commissioned to be a witness, am I more concerned with keeping lesser loyalties? Have I lulled my conscience into believing I am immune to the demands of the gospel, and lacking obedience, found myself in deep trouble?

Pardon my sins of presumption and petty rebellion. Teach me to love Thee, to desire Thee above all else, to wait quietly before Thee until I find Thy peace.

How easily I lose balance and act out of proportion to the Light I have been given. Often I forget. Often I rebel. Often I stumble and fall. Forgive, O God, and let me be counted among those who would rather walk with Thee through storm than with a dozen well-armed soldiers into the tents of iniquity.

Deepen my faith, stir my zeal, bring me to obedient trust. Let Jesus be central in my affections and Thy will foremost in my prayers. Hold me close to Thee. All through the hours of the night, prepare me in sleep for the responsibilities of tomorrow. Through Christ, my King. Amen.

Morning

Generous God, who art beyond the confines of this time and place, yet intimately involved in all that is permitted to happen; I have become increasingly aware of the generous blessings bestowed on me that I was unaware of at the time. Mine is a prayer of Thanksgiving for these back-door blessings:

the business reversal that led to deeper stewardship,
the give and take of a relationship that opened me to
   my behavior;
the death that led me to appreciate life;
the slow recovery that taught me trust;
the challenge that affirmed my beliefs;
the forsaken habit that led me to new self-respect;
the answer to the sought-for question that changed
   my life;
the friend who stood by;
the memory of the fragrance after the rose had died;
the deft remark that changed my thinking;
the parent who will never stop praying for me.

May my life, graced by innumerable benedictions, be lived in gratitude and allowed to be to bless others. Much has been given me, may I share as bountifully as I have received. Keep my eyes on Jesus, my actions informed by the eternal, and my heart sensitive to Thy leading in this time and place. Through The Changeless Savior, Christ Jesus. Amen.

Midday

Loving God,
I recommit my day to Thee.
Permit that I might serve Thee faithfully enough
To draw others to Thee.
Let no false ambition or secret pride,
No exaggerated estimate or self-serving spirit,
No harbored sin or unwarranted desire, abide within me.
Allow that what I accomplish may be so pervaded by
   Thy Spirit
That what I am unable to accomplish may also be enriched
Through life in The Chosen Son. Amen.

Evening

Can silent lips or empty hands, weary minds or aching hearts, still pray to Thee, O God? Can I in distress still find Thee, though I am unable to search in the ways I have previously known? In my extremity art Thou close enough to hear my whispers, to catch the faint murmurs of my breath and the still lingering desires to commune with Thee? Can it be that no look to Thee goes unnoticed, no cry in pain or whisper in darkness goes unheard? I praise Thee, God, for Thou hast not let me go; Thou hast not turned from me; Thou hast not forgotten me in my hour of need.

The source of my strength is in Thee and beside Thee there is none other. I cannot fight the battles of life nor find victory over the temptations that plague me, without Thy strength. Tonight I come, cornered by one major fault, one major weakness where in the heat of temptation I have yielded and done what I should not have done, forsaking the finest that was in me to pursue the worst that might befall me. In retrospect, the reality of my situation falls in around me and leaves me breathless, broken, and ashamed.

Thou, who canst speak through the silence and break through the barriers of my disobedience; forgive and pardon my defection. Cleanse me from my wicked way and bring me to new strength through the cleansing power that faith engenders in Christ Jesus. Amen.

Morning

Almighty and Righteous God, give me to see the needs of my world as they really are, for this is a planet of inequities and extremes. A few control most of the food and natural resources needful for all. Have I hidden from my consciousness the knowledge of thousands starving each day and will not let this reach my heart? Have misery and hunger been reduced to mere statistics for me? Am I so isolated that I cannot visualize these needs in persons I know? Has The Christ of Compassion become lost to the worship of affluence?

Can it be that chandeliers have become more important than rice?

Has fur storage become more important than grain storage?

Has financial acquisition become more important than food distribution?

How many gods do I have before Thee, Lord? Bring me to a wise sharing of my goods so I may heal hurt, distribute food, feed the needy in body and soul. Let nothing prevent me from visualizing

the refugees of Asia and Africa,

the starving of India and South America,

the poor of the United States and Europe.

May mountain shanties, city slums, and fragile lifeboats give me insight into housing conditions that need change. May I be haunted by injustice in whatever form it takes, until I rise from knees bent in prayer to use hands busy in service, helping those who cannot help themselves. May I be convicted by those who ask so little and need so much, to do all I can, as long as I can, in every way that I can, God helping me, until The Kingdom comes. Let it be, Lord Jesus, let it be. Amen.

Midday

I pause at the zenith of this wintry day, Holy God, to find Thee without whom I cannot find the way. Grant me courage to take those paths pleasing to Thee and for the benefit of humanity. May I avoid those paths so widely traveled that emphasize the peripheral, miss the imperative and embrace the secondary. Show me what matters most and allow me to matter in its advancement. For Jesus' sake. Amen.

Evening

Omnipotent and Omnipresent Father, I express appreciation for this nation:
for her religious freedoms;
for her guarantees of individual rights;
for her natural beauty and resources;
for her unlimited opportunities;
for her open gates to foreigners;
for her diversity and strengths;
for her high ideals and valiant efforts to live by them.

I pray for the leaders of this nation, that they may be men and women of high ethical standards and moral leadership.

Uphold my country:
Where she is wrong, nudge her to reform.
Where she is right, increase her wisdom.
Where she is lax, challenge her.
Where she is God honoring, bless her.

Guide all efforts for peace in the world, all who seek the stability of international law, all who work for peace. May Thy righteousness be honored and human life respected in every country.

Lord of Nations, before whom all time and events will one day be consummated, search the hearts and minds of all Thy people and bring us to humbly sing Thy praise. Through The King of Kings, Lord of Lords, Love incarnate. Amen.

Morning

Great God, whose mercy, love, and power is from everlasting to everlasting the same; when I did not come to Thee, Thou camest to me. When I did not acknowledge Thee, did not utter Thy Name nor think to utter Thy Name, even then didst Thou think of me, wast concerned for me and wanted to help me.

Father in Heaven, how shamelessly I forgot Thee and in moments when I did not forget Thee, tried to run from Thee. I have traveled far and wide in my rebellion, only to find Thee waiting there when I reached my destination. I have emphasized peripheral matters and let the essentials of life fall by the wayside.

Examine my heart:

Have I pursued pleasure to the neglect of prayer?
Have I let temptation linger and ignored The Holy Spirit?
Have I failed my family to pacify acquaintances?
Have I read lesser books and overlooked The Book of Life?
Have I seen only myself, my needs and wants, to the exclusion of humanity's pain?
Have I avoided the deep questions of life, to the detriment of my soul?

Father, call me back. Do not let me wander from Thy Purposes. Center me in the faith that purposes my salvation and is committed unreservedly to Christ. May I look above the din and confusion of life and take the clues for my existence from The God of Creation, then through Holy Spirit and Jesus, The Son, be guided this day and every day, and on That Day. Amen.

Midday

Abiding Lord;
Near in quiet of dawn and heat of noonday;
Still me to catch the rhythms of Thy Presence and reflections of Thy will.
Merge my spirit with Thine and alert my heart to Thy revelations.
Calm me to the silence of Thy ways and fill me with the Spirit of Truth.
Through The Unvanquished Mercy.
Amen.

Evening

Gracious Lord, Guide of Life, help of the helpless, support of the faltering, strength of the weary; I do not pray solely for myself but for those who wait: for the doctor, for the letter, for the check, for the results, for the reprieve, for the confirmation, for an opening, for a phone call, for a friend, for acceptance, for food, for help, for relief, for deliverance, for better times, for the end to come.

O Thou, who in the fullness of time sent Thy Son into the world, a Savior acquainted with all our sorrows, stabilize and undergird those who waited and received sad news. Be especially close to those who must deal with:

pain, that does not subside,
sleeplessness, that weakens and frays,
guilt, that haunts and plagues,
fear, that diminishes and divides,
grief, that numbs and hurts,
depression, that immobilizes and ruins,
anger, that cankers and destroys.

Undergird them by the Power beyond their ability to imagine or conceive. Lavish them with Thy generous love. Protect and bless them through the silent hours of the night. Bring all Thy children to breathe Thy Name in prayer through The Christ of Calvary. Amen.

Morning

Blessed and Merciful Lord, whose love is ever present, before whom I feel my sinfulness and inadequacy so acutely; forgive me of these sins that testify more to my weakness than of appropriating Thy grace:

harsh words with scant caring,
greedy pursuits with flippant concern,
envious designs with small notice,
temptation pursued with little regret,
money worshiped without remorse,
demands made with little insight,
prayer avoided with ready excuse,
persons offended with no apology,
stones thrown with no looking back,
criticism leveled with no sensitivity.

Has my behavior made a mockery of my faith? Do I desire to glorify myself to the exclusion of Thy Lordship? Have I lost sight of the forgiving love of God until its life-changing compassion has dimmed from my eyes and effected my relationships? Forgive this usurping pride that grips me more often than I confess. By faith build me, by hope encourage me, by love guide me in the way. Guard me against yielding to temptation. Sanctify me in honorable service. Edify me through the Scriptures. Inform me in prayer. Allow me to end this day as useful and influential in Thy purpose as it was intended to be. Through the power of The Obedient Nazarene. Amen.

Midday

God of Creation,
Who has blessed me with a morning of light and challenge;
Extend Thy mercies into the afternoon that
Working, I may grow in trust of God,
Serving, I may learn humility with others,
Praying, I may couple motivation with grace
To honor The Lord Jesus Christ in all things.
Amen.

Evening

Lord God Omnipotent, before whom all persons will stand in judgment and before whom all nations are weighed in the balances:

> May the Church be wise enough to apply biblical truth to the realities of evil.

> May the ministers and missionaries of the Church, at home and abroad, be undergirded to expound the gospel of salvation.

> May the compassion of the Church bring the light of Christ to the dark places of the world, from wealthy mansions to simple huts.

Give unction to Thy disciples.

Give mercy to those who are persecuted for righteousness' sake.

Give sustenance to those who labor in well-doing.

Set the captives free, minister to the suffering, and increase the spread of the gospel.

Let the Church:
> uphold sound doctrine,
> encourage strong faith,
> overcome petty divisions,
> deepen worship,
> couple love with justice to
> magnify Christ Jesus.
>> Now and always. Amen.

Morning

O God, most Holy, I praise Thee for the day begun and the fullness it affords me to praise Thee. Allow that I may always express authentically what I believe sincerely.

In Thy will is my desire.
In Thy grace is my salvation.
In Thy Word is my succor.
In Thy purpose is my joy.
In Thy love is my sustenance.

How I long to know Thee with purity of purpose, that Thy ways might become familiar to me and I might follow in them. Teach me Thy precepts. Let me love Thy commandments. May my heart desire Thy statutes and my mind feed on Thy Word. I yearn to know Thee better, to sit in Thy Presence, to contemplate Thy judgments and the magnitude of Thy mercy.

Forgive me for living less than I believe and for believing less than, in Thy love, I could know. Lead me to follow Thee in joyful obedience through Jesus, The Savior. Amen.

Midday

Almighty God, I praise Thee for the night of restful sleep, the morning of renewed refreshment and the midday moment of reflection. Help me to live in these busy hours so I will not return to sleep ashamed or guilty. Enable me to make of this day a reality that will resonate with the truths that hold sway in my soul. Lead me to be faithful and honorable in the work I have to do, to marshall from the inside the discernment I need to face the outside, to give more than I receive, to care more than is required, to be honest with myself, compassionate with the needy and loyal to The Living Christ. Amen.

Evening

O Lord, my God, I stand aside and gather up the fragments of my jostled day: the requests, the calls, the reversals, the dilemmas, the limitations, the continuations, the friendly faces, the lonely faces, the uncertain faces. I have walked with ambiguity and paradox. Good and evil have struggled within me. There have been moments when I have lived one way and felt another; there have been times of inner scrutiny when I wondered if this was really the way I wanted to do life. I search to be the person I know I can be.

Allow me to know myself in the love of others, allow others to know themselves in my love. May I look beneath the surface of my days to distinguish the transitory from the eternal and opt for that which builds and does not destroy. Loving Father, keep speaking to me, keep directing me, keep relating me to the fullness of the stature of faith in The Son, my Savior, in whom is my trust and my joy. Amen.

Winter

Winter spells a magic all its own when new fallen snow blankets earth and tree. Bright sunshine marches across long frozen fields where red cardinals fight blue-jays for plump berries along the fence row. There is a quietness about the land when snow envelops and frost inhibits. It is a stillness all its own, a thing separate from the quiet found at any other season of the year. It is a peace to be reckoned with, the deeper one goes, the richer that silence becomes.

In winter the heart turns to introspection, the mind evaluates, the soul contemplates; it has always been so. We are made to slow our pace when weather shoves us indoors. There we can evaluate where we have come from, what we have been doing, where we are going. In winter the thoughtful soul can ask the fundamental questions.

As time would have it a pivotal event approaches, the birthday of a King, Christ Jesus, born centuries ago in Bethlehem of Judea. Nothing could be more needed or welcome in our contemplative quest for the meaning of life than Advent. We soon find out our need for fellowship with God, those of us who see ourselves as we really are, who know the depths of our sinfulness and the limitations of our minds. The Good News of the Inbreak of God in human flesh stirs the mind and moves the soul to worship. Incarnation, from cradle to cross, paves the way for the exercise of faith; we may always come to Him who is always coming to us. It is enough to warm the heart against the winter cold, to stir the soul to new heights of adoration, to catch a glimpse of the mystery of God in our redemption. Perhaps this has been part of the purpose of our Creator all along, for those who brave cold winters. The quiet ways of God are past finding out; they are so rich when they slip up on us.

Morning

Lord God, who hath not always been as revealed to Thy children as Thou art now, who through the Incarnation of Christ Jesus, came and lived among us, undergoing all the trials and burdens we undergo, and wresting victory over sin and death; hear this morning gratitude for the Advent arrival of The Christ Child and for His continuous entry into hearts of faith today.

> Not just a baby in Bethlehem's stable
>> but The King of Kings!
> Not just a lad in a carpenter's shop
>> but The Hope of Israel!
> Not just a teacher on the hillside
>> but The Light of The World!
> Not just a criminal on the cross
>> but the very Son of God!
> Not just an angel on the right hand of Glory
>> but The Resurrected Advocate, forever!

Let me not be callous with the familiar Christmas story. Grant me meekness like those who came from near and far and knelt in the lowly stable to adore the Christ Child. Then, may I arise and walk with the Light of that night and of its Savior into the gaping needs and painful hurts of this world, proclaiming the gospel message of Redemption. In the joy of my Lord. Amen.

Midday

Creator of the morning and the night,
Of noon and afternoon and gentle evening,
As Thou hast led me in the morning,
Guide me in the afternoon.
Stir me to strength commensurate to my opportunities.
Challenge me to service worthy of my devotion.
Lead me to need equal to my resources,
That evening shadows may affirm
What daylight efforts now confirm:
Thou hast led me in this day
And graced me strongly all the way.
Amen.

Evening

Loving God, who in The Spirit and The Son hath taught me my need of Thee and thus to pray, as I visualize the faces of these whom I remember in prayer, may each one in their own way be made unusually aware of Thy Presence this night. Touch those:

who have more than they can handle and face diminished options;

who suffer through wrongs they committed or through wrongs others committed;

who have enough of possessions and not enough of peace;

who have lost a loved one and within a year face the same grief again;

who care for themselves haphazardly, for others marginally, for God nominally, or not at all;

who cannot reconcile a God of love with a body of affliction;

who must wait to get well and are impatient and restless;

who are at the end of the road and must make a decision;

who lacked the environmental and parental blessings to form close personal relationships as adults;

who face retirement with inadequate income and depleted resources;

who pray for deliverance and lack faith to act on the prayer;

who are hardened to the plight of the poor, sold out to the love of money;

who are dying and must come to terms with the inevitable.

Be close to these and all others who need Thee this night and bring us all to call Thy Name in prayer. Through the ever present Christ. Amen.

Morning

My heart is broken, O God, at the waywardness
of my life:
at shattered promises and crumbled possibilities,
at flagrant disobedience and discarded hopes,
at foolish failures and senseless excesses,
at unkept vows and tarnished dreams,
at sincere commitments, shriveled,
because I spread myself too thin.

I attempted more than I could handle and leaning entirely
on myself, ignored Thy counsel; now I lie down drained,
beaten, and worn.

O Lord, forgive me the excesses of overextending
and under-evaluating, of failing to look to Thee, of failing
to count the cost before the commitment and coming
home with half a loaf. Were I to look less at selfish
interests and more at Kingdom concerns, surely I would
learn to make peace with priorities and experience patience in well doing.

Heavenly Father, let me not become overly concerned with my place in the scheme of things. Thou hast
set me in the right place and Thy promise to hold me
cannot be diminished. Loved ones assure me, faith undergirds me, and promise of heaven awaits me at the end
of the road. Calm me in Thy trust, renew me in Thy
grace, and use me in Thy love at a pace in keeping with
Thy will. In Messiah's Name. Amen.

Midday

Shepherd of my soul,
My heart and affections now control.
My mind and will affect,
My steps and actions redirect,
According to Thy will.

Light of my life,
Victor over sin and strife.
Grace of God in Christ proclaimed,
Let my life in Thee remain,
Conforming to Thy will.
Amen.

Evening

Loving Heavenly Father, as I examine my relationships today, help me to do so mindful of the actions of Jesus that can show the way to maturity.

Have I projected onto others behavior I fear in myself?

Have I categorized others to remove my involvement?

Have I accused others to clear my guilt?

Have I expected others to make exceptions for me I did not deserve?

Have I suspected others of deeds I deny?

Have I maintained obsolete prejudices?

Have I in anger spoken too quickly?

Have I required too much, praised too little, and taken it out on the innocent?

Have I wanted security from others that is alone Thy Providence?

Forgive these sins of relationships, intentional or unintentional. Let me face my motives. Let me not be deceived about jealousy and blame placing. Let me be honest with Thee and in restitution to those I have harmed. My mistakes are many and often. May I have the Spirit of The Master who in compassion or rebuke, sinned not, who loved the forgotten and confused as they were meant to be loved. Hear my gratitude for having been included in that love and my resolve to love others more wisely in return. Amen.

Morning

Lord, God, Creator of heaven and earth,
Whose watchcare spans the galaxies yet encompasseth
the human heart,
Whose ways are not my ways,
Whose thoughts are not my thoughts,
Whose justice is sure,
Whose commandments are perfect,
Whose purposes are pure;
Hear Thou my humble prayer.
Grant me freshness of perspective in difficult places,
Allow me acuity of thought in trying situations.
Orient me to spiritual realities amid daily tasks.
Make me aware this day of:
>   the subtle pride of self-pity,
>   the ruinous pride of superiority,
>   the deceptive pride of knowledge,
>   the illusive pride of wealth,
>   the tenuous pride of privilege,
>   the destructive pride of power,
>   the fickle pride of popularity,
>   the devastating pride of religiosity.

Gather me closer to Thee, O Lord, that in Thy
holiness I will distinguish the deceptiveness of pride from
the deep well springs of faith and follow The Christ who
never confused the two. In His Name. Amen.

Midday

Merciful Father, forgive me this day if I have
done or said anything to inflict hurt or pain in the world.
Pardon my curtness, my impatience, my failure to encourage and help when I had the opportunity; and allow me
in the hours that remain, to lessen, not increase, the
burdens that weigh so heavily on human hearts. Through
Jesus Christ, my Lord. Amen.

Evening

Lord, Omnipotent and Holy, whom to know is
life itself, hear my petition:

I pray for those who do not live for others
But live for what others can do for them;
For whom dependence is a lifestyle
And the sun never shines on their responsibility.

I pray for those who know the life of privilege,
Who live to increase their lot;
For whom the plight of the homeless and hungry
    mean little,
And the sun never sets on their vast possessions.

I pray for those who struggle to make ends meet,
Who labor long hours living on limited incomes,
For whom life is difficult yet faith is real,
So the sun never sets apart from their gratitude to
    Thee.

I pray for those who are steeped in religious devotion
But are lax in living divine truth;
For whom ritual is more important than intervention
And the sun never shines on their compassion.

I pray for those who are never sure,
Who search in ambivalence and believe with
    reservation;
For whom all things are relative
And the sun never shines in a peaceful heart.

I do not intercede for these ones out of innocence, O Lord. I recognize in myself those traits that
appear so predominant in them and realize how pitifully
reluctant I am to name my own faults, and work to
overcome them. Allow that I may not follow Thee at a
distance in these matters, but embrace Thee in contrition
and live in pardon. Through the victory of my Lord Jesus
Christ. Amen.

Morning

Kind Heavenly Father, may this day not emerge without the emergence of my praise for the gift of it, for the blessings it bestows, for the challenges it presents, the opportunities it calls me to examine.

Hear my praise for:
> the glory of the dawn,
> the joining of earth brown and patchy white in snowy company,
> the cool, clear crystal of icicles,
> the busy chatter of hungry birds,
> the bright sunshine of winter,
> the warmth of shelter from which to view the landscape,
> the time to anticipate and thus appreciate the coming spring.

Now as I look from the beauty of the day to its opportunities, may I be given wisdom and courage:
> let me forgive that I may learn to love;
> let me sacrifice that I may appreciate;
> let me seek that I may find;
> let me study that I may learn;
> let me appreciate that I may appropriate;
> let me reconcile that I may bring peace;
> let me pray that I may praise God.

In all the day brings, may I bring it all to Thee, my God, and wait in prayer. Let gratitude so fill my soul that I will not be imbalanced by ingratitude. Let my acceptance of this day and my living of it honor Thee in whom is my strength and my joy. Amen.

Midday

Lord God, before whom no secrets are hid, no fears unknown, no sin hidden; give me faith to believe that as I reach for strength, strength will be given; as I ask for wisdom, wisdom will be provided; as I seek righteousness, I will be rewarded accordingly. O Thou, who hast never broken a promise nor failed the faithful, undergird me with strength to serve in the rest of this day as I wanted to do in the first of the day and in tomorrow's light to serve Thee even more fully in Christlike love. Amen.

Evening

Almighty God, the world at large appears before me and I am haunted by the suffering of humanity: the illiterate, the refugee, the leper, the hungry, the blind, the homeless, the mentally and physically handicapped. Help me to apply my faith to the reality at hand.

Mine has often been a detached concern. What value is sleep if with the strength of it I do not help those who cannot sleep due to hunger? What worth is a fine home if I do not help those who are homeless? What satisfaction can there be in fine clothes if I do not share with those who are cold and exposed? Are these not the questions I must face in stewardship of my bounty? Let my compassion be commensurate with my gratitude and my sharing in keeping with the depths of Thy Mercy.

Now in the Name of my Lord Jesus Christ:
    let my head bow in prayer,
    let my will bow in obedience,
    let my heart bow in adoration,

through the Perfect Love that bowed in submission to the Cross, emerged from the tomb triumphant and reigns with Thee forever. Amen.

Morning

God of Revelation and Redemption, whose purpose for me is beyond my understanding but within grasp of my interpreting, I would make today a day of prayer. Knit my soul with Thine. May Jesus become as real in my living as I have come to know Him in my prayers. May I exhibit His Presence as genuinely in public as I know it in private. Almighty God, who art not wanting in mercy nor reluctant to forgive, whose compassion is as full for one as for all; I pray for those who do not pray because:

they do not want to, they have no time,
they are uncomfortable, they do not know how,
they feel it is presumptuous, they doubt,
they are hesitant, or they over-expect and under-
experience.

Let not their reservations stifle the possibility of belief; draw them close to Thyself, even as in Christ, Thou hast drawn me and bring us all, unworthy though we be, to call Thy Name in faith. Amen.

Midday

Eternal Lord, strengthen me in this noon hour to build on that which I have begun. May I be as sensitive to personalities and feelings as I am committed to deadlines and demands. Enable me to go the distance with my task and as much as lies within me, to finish what I have begun. In The Name of Jesus, who finished what began before creation, gifting the world with Life that never ends. Amen.

Evening

I praise Thee, Heavenly Father, for the variety and depth of my relationships with others. May I so represent Thee as to bring no disgrace to the Kingdom in which I belong or The God I represent. May I continually forgive others when they err and may they forgive me when I disappoint them. Allow me to be authentic, never false or fake or overborne with a sense of my importance. Bless those persons who:

laugh, lift, and cheer me;
lead, direct, and bless me;
disagree, challenge, and question me;
prod, encourage, and move me;
love, respect, and need me;
care, sacrifice, and touch me;
write, think, and teach me;
listen, pray, and undergird me.

In stillness and reflection, I catch the words of those who have spoken to me today, voices that echo messages I need to hear, telling me who they are, sharing with me who they believe I am. These are the relationships through whom Thy Spirit breathes and through whom my gratitude rises. Hear also my humble praise for relationship in Christ Jesus, closer than any other relationship and unending. In Thee I am made whole. Amen.

Morning

Merciful and Compassionate Father, I begin my day with thoughts of others who are needy but keep missing the mark:

solvency was theirs, but they overspent;
opportunity was theirs, but they were too busy;
strength was theirs, but they made no effort;
friendship was theirs, but they allowed it to lapse;
beauty was theirs, but they overplayed it;
forgiveness was theirs, but they would not repent;
love was theirs, but they mixed loyalties.

I, too, have lived in self-defeating ways. I have often missed what I needed most because I looked in the wrong places. I have often failed to pray.

May my use of today be one of victory, not defeat. May I have the insight to see what is happening, the humility to ask Thy guidance, the strength to appropriate Thy grace, the courage to believe, and the will to obey, in the Strong Deliverer's Name. Amen.

Midday

Let me be quieted, stilled, and patient in waiting for Thee this noon hour, O Lord, until I can call from within the power to face battles without. Let me know my heart well enough to seek Thy cleansing when I fail and Thy humility when I succeed. Let praise not take me too high nor criticism too low. Let the Living Christ so live in me that what I do and how I do it may point to Thee. Amen.

Evening

Lord of Grace, as I turn in prayer from the hustle and
bustle of the day to the nurture of family and quiet with
Thee, allow me to examine in prayer that which I most
need in living:

Is it patience in waiting?
Is it motivation in work?
Is it strength in temptation?
Is it discipline in speech?
Is it devotion to family?
Is it bridling of temper?
Is it re-examination of priorities?
Is it expansion of faith?
Is it openness to reality?
Is it freedom from worry?
Is it acceptance of grace?
Is it reconciliation in relationships?
Is it perseverance in prayer?

Let this evening examination be a probing and
honest one, for my sins of omission are many and it is
difficult to see where I have missed the way. Where I lack
the strengths Thou callest to mind, grant me the desire for
them and the prayerful determination to work for their
accomplishment. Through The Lord Jesus Christ. Amen.

Morning

Fix my heart, O Lord, on Thee, for all else changes and that which was present passes away and that on which I previously relied is no longer reliable. Those upon whom I placed so much dependence have gone another way and are no longer available. Everything has changed. The weather is not the same; new things are now faded and old and I am grown old also. Where am I to turn in this world of shifting and change? Where is that upon which I can rely, which time will not erase nor circumstance alter?

I come to Thy Word, whose precepts are given for my instruction, in whose obedience alone is true freedom. Is this not reality no age or event can alter? Let me obey Thy commandments, adhere to Thy prophecy, follow Thy wisdom and internalize Thy gospel which knows my heart better than I.

Let me not be so tethered by change as to diminish my trust of Thee or to doubt for one moment Thy love for me. Hide me in Christ Jesus, The Solid Rock, before whom the shifting tides of history are as passing waves against the seashore of eternity. Amen.

Midday

Lord, allow me to live
Amid the heartbreak and strife
Of this complex world,
With resolute hope and brave faith.
And grant that when my journey is over
I will have given more than I received,
Forgiven more than was forgiven me,
And hoped more than I ever thought possible,
Through life in The Self-emptying Son.
Amen.

Evening

Holy God, as I enter into this evening time of intercession and come to those moments when I place faces with needs, calling private names of fellow pilgrims in prayer; do uphold and aid them, comfort and strengthen them, heal and restore them according to Thy will. And if I may be a part of the healing process, let me do so humbly, quietly, prayerfully, in the Name of Jesus.

I pray for the sick in body and mind who prefer it that way:

> for the birth defected who need constant care;
> for the teenage depressed who are suicidal;
> for the refugees and homeless whose temporary misery has become permanent;
> for the paranoid who cannot come too close;
> for the able-bodied jobless who struggle to hold together;
> for the aged and senile who feel useless and unwanted and have evidence to back this up;
> for the schizophrenics who have trouble getting the parts together;
> for the victims of crime and the victims of judicial injustice;
> for the promiscuous who have misused their love and feel it is too late to change;
> for the apprehensive and nervous who cannot control their tension;
> for the poor and hungry who see no way out;
> for prisoners in cells of their own making who will not use their keys.

Guard and keep all who suffer, and let Thy mercy flow to them unabated. For Jesus' sake. Amen.

Morning

Lord, of this age and every age, to whom past, present, and future are as one, who seest the long march of human history from beginning to end and stretchest forth Thy hand in love to mark the passage;

May my work today, light or demanding,
    be faithfully performed;
May my relationships, deep or passing,
    be caring and appropriate;
May my mind, alert or tired,
    be reminded of Thy precepts
    and loyal to Thy commandments.

A day is a precious gift and I would be a responsible steward. May I exhibit love:
    that perceives, but does not reject;
    that evaluates, but does not condemn;
    that suffers with, but does not forsake;
    that pursues, but does not coerce;
    that appreciates, but does not take advantage;
    that cares, but does not overwhelm.

For it is in the expression of love that I can be most like Thee, who first loved me and through the Son, hath given me everlasting life. I praise Thee for the Love that had room for one more, and still does! Amen.

Midday

Merciful and Compassionate God, I am prone to hiding, given to secrecy, fond of excuses, and driven by sin to deny Thee and thus need Thee all the more. I thank Thee that no matter how far I wander, Thou art not far away. Let me not forsake Thy judgment. May I be quick to repent and fast to appropriate Thy forgiving grace. May my faith be strong enough to share with one who is enduring intense tribulation, that grace may balance witness in honor of The Advocate Son. Amen.

Evening

Why is it, Lord, I acknowledge with my heart the
Resurrection and live as though it never happened? Why
proclaim one thing in worship and live another in daily
life? Why act in concert with Thy power one day and
forsake Thy entreaties the next? I grapple with this di-
chotomy that tears at my soul. I know the price of my
salvation; I know the tomb is empty and still I falter.
Temptation confronts me and suddenly that which I could
handle becomes too much for me; faith tested in the fire of
pressure, melts away. I am left discouraged, despairing.
Yet the vestiges of truth remain; they are with me day and
night and I would find no peace at all, were it not for the
persistence of Thy Love that outlasts the dark night and
trying day.

Bring me to a place of obedient trust. Flood Thy
gracious power upon me. Steady my soul; arm me with
the helmet of salvation, the shield of faith and the sword
of The Word, that I may stand strong in the evil day
through the express image of The Invisible God: Christ
Jesus. Amen.

Morning

Almighty God, in whose love and watchcare I begin and end and journey through my day, I bow before Thee in contrition and reverence for Thou hast ordered my days and knowest the intent of my heart in living them. May the presence of Jesus so pervade my heart that I may love Thee and my neighbor with the depth of love with which I love myself.

I celebrate with those for whom this day is a first:
> a first day of marriage, in a new home or with their firstborn;
> a first day of vacation, or in a new job or of an unexpected friendship;
> a first day out of the hospital, in a new location or as a confessing Christian.

I am mindful of those who would give so much to be initiated into the privileges that others so routinely accept. My gratitude overflows for the blessings that surround my life, let my stewardship be commensurate with my appreciation. Allow in those areas I do not and may never experience, that I may see beyond the present to the Kingdom that is to come, be content with a simple lot, and labor to honor my God through The Humble Savior. Amen.

Midday

Lord, I pause between the fresh pace of the morning
And the slackened pace of the afternoon
To ponder the passage of the day:
> Challenge me where I have faltered.
> Encourage me where I have despaired.
> Strengthen me where I am weak.

For often I look and compare and envy another;
I toil and labor and give up too soon;
I over-invest and over-expect and become mired in frustration.
Quiet me within that I may lessen requests,
Regroup resources and integrate the life of Christ. Amen.

Evening

Holy God, most compassionate and wise, given to long-suffering and patience; I come to Thee tonight bearing the grievous weight of my divisive nature, realizing how easy it is for me to proclaim one thing and live another. I find myself guilty of:

> expecting deliverance and prodding temptation;
> acknowledging wealth and ignoring poverty;
> condoning armaments and condemning war;
> harboring hate and pretending acceptance;
> admiring avarice and disavowing greed;
> straddling the fence and blaming the past;
> increasing the problem and denying my part;
> risking little and wanting much.

Merciful God, I am undone by the magnitude of my sins. I find I have excluded Thee at the very points I need Thee most. Melt my defensiveness, heal my turmoil. May I less and less pursue the empty enticements of evil and more and more conform to the demands of the faith, through which Christ shares His liberating pardon in love. Amen.

Morning

Lord God, I adore Thee, I praise Thee, I magnify Thee, for Thou hast chosen to deal with me not after what I deserve but out of Thy inexhaustible grace. When I did not acknowledge Thee nor utter Thy Name, nor think to utter Thy Name, even then Thou didst think of me, wast concerned for me, wanted to assist me. How shamelessly I forgot Thee, tried to run from Thee, tried to set up a place apart from Thee, only to find in arriving Thou hadst been there all along.

O Thou, destination of all human souls, counsel on my right hand and protection on my left; I live in the light of Thy Providence; Thy grace toward me is great and Thy understanding as deep as the sea. In Thine own initiative Thou didst draw me into the circle of Thy love and I have found home. I praise Thee, I magnify Thee, I glory in Thy mighty deeds and Thy great salvation in Christ Jesus, my Redeemer. Amen.

Midday

May the problems of this day not overwhelm me, Lord. Give me to know the grace equal to all I may face now and reliable for eternity. Grant me perspective in perplexity, patience in trial, and strength in adversity through the power of The Holy Spirit. Amen.

Evening

Generous God, incline Thine ear to my evening gratitude:

    for a life full of variety and possibility;
    for a mind of learning and curiosity;
    for a body of health and energy;
    for a soul of sensitivity and searching;
    for friends of objectivity and depth;
    for a world of intricacy and beauty;
    for opportunities that broaden and deepen;
    for loved ones that require and inspire;
    for challenges that search and test;
    for the Word that orients and convicts;
    for the Spirit that illumines and guides.

      I have been greatly blessed. Thy generosity has been lavished upon me. Each day is full of new potentials and laden with options. My blessings are as innumerable as the sands of the sea. May I not waste what I have been given. May I not take lightly my stewardship nor shirk my responsibilities. Let me be found in the activities of each day as Jesus was found during his days on earth, alert to human need and spiritual reality, able to relate the two in redemptive ways. May courageous faith grapple with the disorder, chaos, and pain of the world. Allow The Christ of Calvary to so pervade my mind and actions that gratitude will blossom into service which speaks of a Kingdom, a King, and a great salvation. Amen.

Morning

Omnipotent God, who understands my needs before I ask, who has provisioned me with daily bread, a measure of health and emerging faith; I intercede for those who meet today with sadness. Take me out of myself for a while to consider their distress. They are uncertain how much longer they can endure, for they are perplexed by: a boring job, incriminating evidence, an unwanted debt, limited income, constant threats, a defeating marriage, a bad reputation, severe addiction, parental responsibility, a plaguing handicap, institutionalization, imprisonment, a noisy apartment, an incurable illness, declining health, a guilty conscience.

Open my eyes to their need, and allow me to assist them as I am able in accordance with Thy will.

Though there are many for whom today is a trying day, I thank Thee for that which undergirds me in life and that which blesses me beyond measure:

the spell of good books;
the power of drama;
the inspiration of music;
the lilt of laughter;
the quickening of thought;
the freshness of flowers;
the turning seasons;
the joy of imagination;
the fulfillment of giving;
the love of family;
the fellowship of God.

From the struggles I have overcome and the blessings I have received, let me make of my day a gift of gratitude and strong hope. Through Jesus Christ, to whom with Thee and the Holy Spirit belongs the praise and the glory forever. Amen.

Midday

Gracious Lord, Thou knowest how easy it is for me to judge others in lights I am unwilling to turn on myself; how quickness to criticize and fastness to condemn come easily to the impatient mind. Allow me grace to repent my hastiness and patience to appropriate Thy pardon lest I project my petty guilt on others and deny the cleansing power of The Forgiving Son. Amen.

Evening

Great and Holy God, whose concern is for all and whose mercy is unending:

if I cry out in grief and pain;
if I come in moral perplexity;
if I seek with a divided heart;
if I call in time of heartache;
if I turn to Thee and cannot find the words;
if I am ashamed and guilty;
if I need Thee and feel my unworthiness;

then look with mercy upon me and send Holy Spirit to aid me. Often I am far from Thy will and I cannot find the way. Often I am overwhelmed in pride and rebellion. Often the world closes in and sorrow dampens my spirit. Often I would know Thee better but am discontent to wait, to pray, to search the stillness and contemplate the Word.

By Thy power bring me to repentance
and restore my soul.

By Thy power comfort me in sorrow
and undergird my spirit.

By Thy power show me the straight and narrow path
that personifies Thy righteousness.

By Thy power release me from all that parts me from
Thee, and return joy to my soul.

I am thankful that as the night surrounds me, my soul is joined with Thine in closer, deeper company. Fill me in sleep with realizations of Thy sanctifying power and protecting Providence. Then, Lord, embolden me to live tomorrow in the courage of The Poured-Out Life of Christ. Amen.

Morning

Holy God, boundless in blessing and mercy,
Who art not slack nor slow of purpose,
Give me to see more nearly as Thou doest see
The world in which I live.
May I not falter where Thou canst renew
Nor fail where Thou canst conquer.
Strengthen my faith in Thee until
I live more in trust than vacillation
And am conformed to Thy will.

Hear my gratitude for big messages wrapped in small
packages:
   a child's hand in mine,
   the echo in a seashell,
   a good night's sleep,
   the order of a beehive,
   a squirrel planting acorns,
   a picnic bench by the river,
   Holy Communion,
   red tulips nodding spring rain,
   a faithful dog,
   receiving a nicely wrapped gift,
   the intricacy of snowflakes,
   the steadiness of the seasons,
   the direction tree limbs point.

Cause me to look and listen beneath the surface
for signs of Thy glory passed and blessing bestowed for
Thou art generous beyond measure and were I to spend
all my days praising Thee it would not be praise enough.
Through the gift of The Nazarene, I pray. Amen.

Midday

Lord,
Grant me the grace to love Thee with a whole heart;
That in pursuing Thee I may find Thee;
In finding Thee I may serve Thee;
In serving Thee where others need Thee,
I may exemplify the Love that found me
And seeks us all for Jesus' sake. Amen.

Evening

Almighty God,
Who hast sustained me through the long hours of the day
And hast created me needy of a night of rest,
I come relinquishing my conscious hold
On all the vexations and challenges of the day,
Desirous to embrace the ways of sleep.

How easily I forget what others have done for me assum-
    ing I accomplish most things alone.
How slyly does the conviction overtake me that I need
    more than I possess.
How quickly do I conclude that I am of more importance
    than others around me.
How craftily is the word circulated that without me the
    whole enterprise would collapse.
How alluring the rationale that I must experience most
    things or be limited the rest of my life.

Loving Lord, draw me close enough to Thee to catch the
    perspective of Thy will.
Fortify me to face reality neither overrating nor under-
    rating myself.
Allow me insight enough to know my limitations and
    strength enough to affirm my gifts.
Make me perceptive enough to recognize the fallacies of
    half-truth
And wise enough to cling to the eternalities of Living
    Truth.
Keep me sane and sensible, level-headed, reality-
    oriented, faith-committed and Christ-directed.
In The Master's Holy Name. Amen.